A EUROTON

SIMPLE JAPANESE

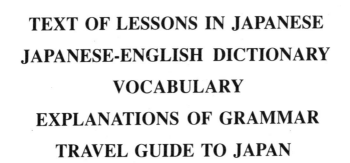

TEXT OF LESSONS IN JAPANESE
JAPANESE-ENGLISH DICTIONARY
VOCABULARY
EXPLANATIONS OF GRAMMAR
TRAVEL GUIDE TO JAPAN

by

Fusako Omori, B.A.
Tōhoko Gakuin University, Sendai City, Japan
Diploma (TESL) Pennysilvania State University,
U.S.A.

EUROPHONE LANGUAGE CENTRE LTD
13 Old Square Lincoln's Inn London WC2A 3UA

Europhone Language Institute (Pte) Ltd.
#04-33 Peninsula Shopping Centre
Coleman Street
Singapore 0617

Europhone Language Institute
122 Campbell Shopping Complex (1st Floor)
Kuala Lumpur

Europhone Language Centre (Pte) Ltd.
13 Old Square Lincoln's Inn
London, WC2A 3UA

5th Edition, 1991

ISBN 9971-994-00-3

CONTENTS

FROM THE AUTHOR

This course has been developed for the person who wants to acquire a basic knowledge of the Japanese language in a short time. It is designed to give you a good foundation in Japanese through proper study materials and the use of everyday, practical conversations. The lessons are generally based on conversational situations such as shopping, meeting people, eating at a restaurant and so on. The stress is not only on grammatical accuracy but also on actual sentence patterns in Japanese.

Arrangement of the Course

The text is divided into ten lessons each of which has three sections. Part I is a dialogue in modern, standard spoken Japanese. A translation of it is given in English. Part II is a bi-lingual vocabulary list. Part III comprises notes on Japanese grammar. This arrangement will be especially helpful to people who want to study on their own. To help you master spoken Japanese quickly, all lessons have been recorded.

Recommendation

We strongly recommend that you devote sufficient time to pronunciation by using the cassettes containing the reading of the lessons by native Japanese. On listening to the tape of the opening dialogue, you can feel the flow of conversation between native speakers. You should spend an hour a day on study. Repeat the sentences and phrases in a clear voice. Frequent listening and repeating is essential to master Japanese. You should learn as many Japanese words as possible. Use the Vocabulary in each Lesson. Word power ensures better understanding and speaking of Japanese. Remember to learn essential grammar to enable you to construct your own sentences.

Fusako Omori
Author

USERS OF OUR COURSES

SOME UNIVERSITIES, COLLEGES, SCHOOLS AND ORGANISATIONS WORLDWIDE WHICH USE EUROPHONE LANGUAGE COURSES

UNIVERSITIES
Srinakhrinwiron University, Thailand
University of Oregon, USA
University of Medison, Wisconsin, USA
University of Malaya
University of Technology
University Sains Malaysia, Penang
University of Singapore
University of Brunei, Darussalam

HIGH SCHOOLS
Kong Yiong High School
Presbyterian High School
Hai Sing Girls High School
St Theresa's High School
Chung Hwa High School
Tuan Mong High School
Anglican High School

SECONDARY SCHOOLS
Willow Avenue Secondary School
Westlake Secondary School
Woodlands Secondary School
Naval Base Secondary School
Boon Lay Secondary School
Yuan Ching Secondary School
Manjusri Secondary School
Tanjong Katong Girls' School
Victoria School
Yuying Secondary School
New Town Secondary School
Whampoa Secondary School
Telok Kurau Secondary School
Sekolah Menengah
    Alirshad, Pow
Sekolah Menengah Sultanah
Shuqun Secondary School

INTERNATIONAL ORGANISATIONS
New Zealand High Commission, Singapore
UNESCO, Bangkok
Telecoms, Singapore
Foreign Language Pte Ltd, Melbourne
Intertaal, Amsterdam
Asian Inst of Technology, Bangkok
POSB, Singapore
Ministry of Defence, Singapore
Petronas, Malaysia
Arab-Malaysian Development Bank
Arkib Negara, Malaysia
Sime Darby Planatations Bhd
Dunlop Malaysian Industry
Shell Malaysia Sdn Bhd
Canadian High Commission (KL)
American Embassy, Thailand

COLLEGES AND INSTITUTES
Institute Piawian Dan Penyelidikan
Forest Research Institute
Institute Penyelidikan dan Pertanian
Institute Technology Mara
Maktab Kerjasama Malaysia
SEAMO Regional Centre, Penang
Institute Perdagangan Mara
Ngee Ann Polytechnic
Institute Kemahiran Mara, PJ (MARA)
Vocational & Industrial Training Board

PRIMARY SCHOOLS
Yuqun Primary School
Jin Tai Primary School
Qifa Primary School
Poi Ching Primary School
Beatty Primary School
Fuchun Primary School
Nan Hua Primary School
Beng Wan Primary School
Haig Boys' Primary School

WELCOME TO JAPAN

Location

Dai Nippon or Land of the Rising Sun is Japan. It's a constitutional monarchy bounded in the North by the Sea of Okhotsk, on the East by the Pacific Ocean, in the South by the East China Sea and on the West by the Sea of Japan. The Japanese islands lie between latitude 28°N and latitude 45° 30'N and longitude 128° 30'E and longitude 146°E.

The Country

Four large islands, seven smaller and one thousand lesser ones constitute Japan. The largest are Hokkaido, Honshu, Shikoku and Kyushu. The total land area is 142,672 square miles. The main island, Honshu is about 200 miles at its broadest while the coastline of Japan is 15,500 miles long. A country of high mountains, valleys and small plains, only 18% of the land is cultivable. Many rivers, the longest of which is the Shinano, flow out of the valleys of Honshu.

Japan has the highest yield per acre of cultivable land in the world. Consequently, it is almost self-sufficient in food. Water power harnessed to capacity produces sufficient electricity and water for irrigation and human consumption. Mineral resources are lacking and have to be imported.

Climate

As the country extends through 17° of latitude, the climate differs considerably according to the location. Mean temperatures vary between 40°F on Hokkaido and 60°F in Okinawa. Summers are short and winters severe especially in Hokkaido and north of Honshu; Shikoku, Kyushu and South Honshu have hot and humid summers and mild winters with a little snow.

The People and Cities

The population of Japan is close to 122 million. Tokyo is the largest city with a population in excess of 12 million. It is the hub of commercial, industrial and financial activities. Other important cities are Osaka (6 million), a port and airline terminal, Yokohama (5 million), a shipbuilding centre, Nagoya (4 million), a manufacturing centre and Kobe (3 million), a shipbuilding and transportation centre.

Culture

Early influence came from China and Korea as can be seen in Japanese literature, art and music. Western influence began when the Japanese made contact with the West, especially in the 19th Century.

The principal religions practised are Buddhism, Shinto (worship based on ancestor and nature worship) and Christianity. In the late 19th century, Shinto was a state religion with the worship of the Emperor as God. There was belief in the racial superiority of the Japanese. After the 2nd World War, in 1946 Emperor Hirohito renounced his claims to divinity. The new constitution of 1947 withdrew state support for Shinto and re-introduced freedom of worship.

The illiteracy rate in Japan is less than 2%. The study of English is encouraged and education, up to secondary level, is compulsory. There are over 50 national and 80 private universities. Of the former the University of Tokyo is the largest and of the latter, Nihon and Waseda, which are also in Tokyo.

The Economy

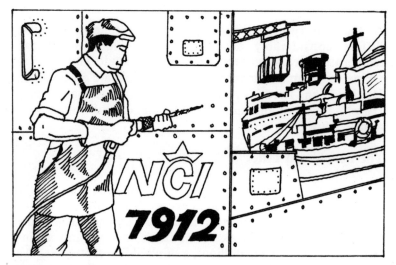

Work in progress.

After the 2nd World War Japan became a major industrial power and graduated from light industries to heavy and chemical industries. Most of its manufactured goods are exported and have helped it to attain an annual GNP only second to the US in the non-communist world. Its trade surplus for last year was nearly US$100 billion.

Agriculture continues to be an important economic activity with over 21,800 sq. miles under cultivation, half of it being devoted to rice growing. Other important crops include wheat, barley, soyabeans, cabbages, onions and oranges.

Manufacturing is the mainstay of the economy. Japan is a leading shipbuilder and manufacturer in the world particularly in electrical products, steel and motor vehicles. About 45% of Japan's exports are derived from the machine industry. Light industrial products include television sets, cameras, optical goods, transistors, computers and automation equipment.

Government

Officers of the Government at work.

In 1889 the first modern constitution was adopted with the supreme executive power being vested in the Emperor. In 1926 Emperor Hirohito ascended the throne as the 124th in the succession which is hereditòry and descends only in the male line. In 1947 a new constitution was formulated by the Japanese and the Allied occupation authorities. The emperor was recognized as the symbol of the nation. Legislative power was exercised by the House of Peers (hereditory peers) and a House of Representatives elected by male Japanese voters. The Emperor appointed the ministers who formed the Cabinet and were responsible to him.

The present Diet (highest organ of government power) consists of a House of Representatives (lower house) and a House of Councillors (upper house) all of whose members are elected. The country is divided into 47 administrative areas (prefactures) which contain municipalities each of which has a legislature made up of elected members. The muncipalities levy taxes and are responsible for public education.

Europhone Research Unit

YOUR FORTUNE IN TOURISM

A fortune awaits businessmen who learn to deal with Japanese tourists. They are arriving by the millions. Last year one million Japanese visited Hong Kong; 800,000 went to Taiwan and 540,000 to Singapore. The annual increase in their numbers is expected to be 10 to 15 percent.

They Don't Speak English

For two days, 120 participants from the tourist industry discussed these findings at a seminar co-sponsored by the Singapore Tourist Promotion Board. One delegate reported, "the ordinary Japanese hardly speaks any English." How then does one deal with them?

Their Expectations

Dr Kuniya, manager of the Japan Travel Bureau Foundation advised, "learning to speak their language helps." The immediate need then is to learn Japanese. Dr Kuniya further clarified that a sympathetic response to the tourists when they are explaining their requirements is important. Ask them to draw a sketch of the article they want, if you do not understand them. They expect efficient and polite service.

Their Profile

The average age of the male tourist is 40 to 49 years. Soon single working women in their 20s are expected to match the men in number. They travel in groups and are careful about hygiene and security. They like fixed price stores as they are not accustomed to bargaining. They do not tip as they consider it impolite.

How to Make a Sale

Let the tourists browse on their own at your shop. Do not

approach them immediately. It makes them uncomfortable. Advise them about your products only after they have picked them up. Offer them alternatives if they are unsuitable. Do not boast or deride your competitors. Be helpful in every way.

Their Favourite Purchases

A common men's item is crocodile skin handbags for wives. For their colleagues they buy belts, ties and pens. Scarfs are for their female staff. They collect souvenirs; *Risis* orchids are very popular. The ladies like shoes with well known brand names. Stockings and handbags in white, black, grey or navy blue colour are in demand.

Best Cassette Courses

Equipped with this knowledge and skill in speaking Japanese, you will be more successful in dealing with Japanese tourists. For bigger and better language courses, see us at our show-rooms or write to us about our courses in 50 languages.

Sales Manager

THE JAPANESE LANGUAGE

Origin

Along with Korean, Manchu, Mongolian and Turkish, Japanese is considered by many scholars to be part of the Altaic family of languages. It differs from the Indo-European languages in that it is sometimes vague and imprecise. For example with regard to visual impressions, the Japanese word **aoi** may mean green, blue or pale. However, it meticulously describes auditory and tactile impressions.

Vocabulary

Japanese vocabulary was very limited until the 3rd century when a great many Chinese words were borrowed. The number of Chinese words in present-day Japanese far exceeds native Japanese words. In more recent times, European words, in particular English, have been absorbed. This process gained further impetus after the 2nd World War. The language has 5 vowels (**a, i, u, e, o**) and 19 consonants (**k, s, sh, t, ch, ts, n, h, f, m, y, r, w, g, z, j, d, b, p**). The order of words in a sentence is usually that of subject, object and verb. The language has a large number of respectful, honorific and humilific words.

Written Japanese — Kanji

There was no writing system until about 1500 years ago when Chinese characters or ideograms were introduced by Chinese and Korean scholars. The characters called Kanji could not often be used for the highly inflected Japanese words. By the 8th Century A.D., Chinese characters were used as phonetic symbols. These characters were abbreviated in the 9th Century to form 2 Kana syllabries called Katakana and Hiragana. Kana means a symbol that represents a syllable. At first only Kana was used for writing Japanese. Gradually a system evolved for the use of Kanji whenever possible.

Hiragana and Katakana

Usually Hiragana (phonetic symbols written in cursive style) is used for native words and word endings whereas Katakana (phonetic symbols written in angular style) is used for writing imported Western words. The latter is also used in telegrams and official documents. The need to use Chinese characters resulted in the adoption of a substantial number of Chinese words into the Japanese vocabulary. After the 2nd World War, the number of Chinese characters was reduced to 1850 to simplify the written language. These characters were adopted by law and Japanese publications limit themselves to using only these characters (except for the writing of names). 881 of these characters are learnt during the six years of elementary education. The remaining 969 characters are taught in secondary schools. In 1951, 92 characters were added to the list for the writing of Japanese personal names

Kanji Characters

Kanji Character	Romanised Word	Meaning
ichi	one
ni	two
san	three
shi	four

Notes on Grammar

The following points are basic and in most cases reflect differences between the grammar of Japanese and that of English or other European languages.

1   Japanese nouns have neither gender nor number. But plurals of certain words can be expressed by the use of suffixes.

2   The verb generally comes at the end of the sentence or clause.

> e.g. **Watashi wa Tanaka** *desu*. I *am* Tanaka.
> **Watashi wa Kyoto e** *ikimasu*. I *go* to Kyoto.

3   The conjugation of verbs is not affected by gender, number or the person of the subject.

4   Verb conjugations use only two tenses, the present form and the past form. The use of the present form refers to habitual action or the future. The past form is equivalent to the English past tense, present perfect tense or past perfect tense and can be determined from the context.

5   Adjectives of one type are inflected to show the present and the past tenses. Another type expresses affirmative and negative meanings.

6   The grammatical function of nouns is indicated by particles. Their role is similar to English prepositions, but since they always come after the word, they are sometimes referred to as postpositions.

> e.g. **Tokyo de,** at Tokyo   **Ku-ji ni,** at 9:00
> **Jugo-nichi ni,** on the 15th of the month

7   Many degrees of politeness are expressable in Japanese. In this book the style is one which anyone may use without being impolite.

Director of Studies

YOUR TEACHERS

The following teachers have participated in the recording of this course.

Miss Fusako Omori
B.A., Tohoko Gakin University,
Sendi City, Japan Diploma (TESL)
Pennysilvania State University, USA
Teacher and Author

Mr. Kokubo Hiroshi
B.A., Tokyo University of
Foreign Studies, Japan
B.E., Tokyo Gakugei University, Japan
Qualified Native Speaker

Miss Sandra Hurst
B.A. (Hons), PGCE,
Warrick University, UK
Qualified Speaker of English

PRONUNCIATION

Using Book or Cassette

Learners using the   cassettes of this package will have complete assistance in pronunciation. They should listen to the spoken *sentences* (Part 1) and *vocabulary* (Part 2) of each Lesson and speak in imitation in the short pauses that follow. Repeated practice will produce good results. Learners relying on only the book may use the following guide to pronunciation.

Definitions

A syllable is a unit of the spoken language. *Vowels* are combined with *consonants* to form *syllables* on which pronunciation is based. Pronunciation is the way in which language is spoken.

Vowels

In Japanese there are 5 vowels:
a   i   u   e   o
Long vowels (often represented as ā ii, ū, ē and ō in some texts) are twice as long as short vowels. It is necessary to give long vowels their true value.

Letters		Approximate Pronunciation
a	as in	*calm* but short
e	as in	*net*
i	as in	*key* but short
o	as in	*paw* but short
u	as in	*boon* but short

Semivowel

Vowels combine with consonants to become syllables which are the language units for Japanese pronunciation. The basic vowels and syllables are given below.

a	i	u	e	o
ka	ki	ku	ke	ko
sa	shi	su	se	so
ta	chi	tsu	te	to-
na	ni	nu	ne	no
ha	hi	fu	he	ho
ma	mi	mu	me	mo
ya	—	yu	—	yo
ra	ri	ru	re	ro
wa	(w)i	—	(w)e	(w)o

Consonants

b	as in	*bull*		**n**	as in	*nine*
ch	as in	*chuck*		**p**	as in	*pain*
d	as in	*dull*		**r**	as in	*ran*
f	as in	*fool*		**s**	as in	*sane*
g	as in	*good*		**sh**	as in	*share*
h	as in	*hand*		**t**	as in	*tiger*
j	as in	*J*ack		**ts**	as in	*bits*
k	as in	*kit*		**w**	as in	*ware*
m	as in	*mite*		**z**	as in	*zone*

Special Sounds

1 **g** is pronounced as *good* when it appears initially but in the middle of a word it becomes **ng**, as in *song*.

2 **s** is pronounced as in *sane*, like in the English **s** before the letters **a**, **u**, **e** and **o**. It becomes **sh** before **i**.

3 **z** is like **j** in *Jim* before the vowel **i**.

4 **t** is like **t** in English when it appears before the vowels **a**, **e** or **o**. It becomes **ts** as in *bits* before **u** and **ch** as in *chuck* before the vowel **i**.

5 Double consonants must be pronounced clearly, stopping momentarily after the first.

6 Vowels **i** and **u** are devocalized when they appear after a voiceless consonant, eg **gozaimasu** is pronounced **gozaimas**.

Counter Readings for Cassette(s)

For easy winding of the cassette to the Lesson you wish to study, the cassette player's Counter Readings are given.

Counter Readings for Cassette(s)

Lessons	1	2	3	4	5	6	7	8	9	10
Single Cassette	Side A 0	49	93	153	224	Side B 0	59	117	195	293
Cassette No 1 Two Cassettes	Side A 0	76	Side B 0	77	Cassette No. 2 Side A 0	73	159	Side B 0	81	185

HOW TO USE THIS COURSE

Aims

This course has been developed to enable you to acquire a basic knowledge of Japanese in a short time. It is designed to give you a good foundation through study materials and the use of everyday, practical conversations.

Course Make-Up

The text is divided into ten selected lessons each of which has three sections. Part One is a dialogue in modern spoken Japanese. A translation of it is given in English. Part Two is a Japanese-English vocabulary list. Part Three comprises notes on Japanese grammar. In these sections you have all the essentials to learn

Japanese. To help you master spoken Japanese all the lessons have been recorded in audio-cassettes.

Method

First listen to Lesson 1 on the cassette. Let the teacher read. Follow the written sentences in the book. Stop the cassette at the end of each lesson. Rewind and play the cassette again from the beginning. Speak after the teacher, phrase by phrase or sentence by sentence in the pauses provided. Do this several times with each paragraph until you are satisfied with your pronunciation as compared with the model voices. Then move on to a new paragraph. Proceed in this manner.

Next study the Vocabulary, Translations and Explanations of each Lesson. Read, think and learn the Japanese words and their meanings. Words are important for your speech and the understanding of other people. Learn as many words as you can. Understand the rules of grammar so that you can make your own sentences. Study a little everyday. Don't forget to revise.

Practise speaking Japanese in the beginning with your cassettes, later with people. Make this a habit. Your success with Japanese is assured.

Pronunciation

Should you have this book without cassettes, read the page on *Pronunciation* for your guidance.

Academic Advisory Board

IKKA

Lesson 1   Hajimemashite (How do you do?)

Mr. Hayashi introduces Mr. Yamamoto to Mr. Tanaka.

Hayashi:	**Konnichiwa, Tanaka-san.**
Tanaka:	**Konnichiwa.**
Hayashi:	**Kochira wa Yamamoto-san desu.**
Yamamoto:	**Hajimemashite. Watashi wa Yamamoto desu.**
Tanaka:	**Hajimemashite. Nihon ginkō no Tanaka desu.**
	Kore wa watashi no meishi desu. Dōzo yoroshiku.
Yamamoto:	**Arigatō gozaimasu. Watashi no meishi desu. Dōzo.**
Tanaka:	**Yamamoto-san wa gishi desu ka.**

1

Yamamoto:	Hai, sō desu. Tōkyō Denki no gishi desu. Aa, Tanaka-san kore wa Suzuki no shōkaijō desu.
Tanaka:	Dōmo. Suzuki-san wa ogenki desu ka.
Yamamoto:	Ee, totemo genki desu.

Translation

Hayashi:	Hello, Mr. Tanaka.
Tanaka:	Hello.
Hayashi:	This is Mr. Yamamoto.
Yamamoto:	How do you do? My name is Yamamoto.
Tanaka:	How do you do? I'm Tanaka from Nihon Bank. This is my business card. I'm very glad to meet you.
Yamamoto:	Thank you very much. This is my business card, please.
Tanaka:	Are you an engineer, Mr. Yamamoto?
Yamamoto:	Yes. I'm an engineer at Tōkyō Electric. Oh, Mr. Tanaka, this is Mr. Suzuki's letter of introduction.
Tanaka:	Thanks. Is Mr. Suzuki well?
Yamamoto:	Yes, he is very well.

Vocabulary

konnichiwa	hello, good afternoon
Tanaka	a Japanese surname
san	Mr. Mrs. Miss (suffix)
kochira	this one (implies this person)

2

wa	as for (topic marker, particle)
Yamamoto	a Japanese surname
desu	is, are, am
hajimemashite	How do you do?
watashi	I
nihon	Japan
ginkō	bank
no	-'s (possessive particle)
kore	this
watashi no	my
meishi	business card
dōzo yoroshiku	please favour me
arigatō gozaimasu	thank you very much
dōzo	please
gishi	engineer
ka	particle, question marker
hai/ee	yes
sō desu	that's right
Tōkyō Denki	Tokyo Electric (company name)
aa	oh
Suzuki	a Japanese surname
shōkaijō	letter of introduction
dōmo	very (thank you very much)
genki/ogenki (polite)	in good health
totemo	very

1

Explanations

1. **Greetings**

ohayō gozaimasu	**konnichiwa**
good morning	good afternoon
konbanwa	**oyasumi nasai**
good evening	good night

   sayōnara – good-bye

2. **Hajimemashite**

   Salutation used on meeting a person for the first time.

3. **Dōzo yoroshiku**

   This means *I am glad to meet you,* and is usually combined with **hajimemashite** when you are introduced to someone for the first time.

4. **Tanaka-san**

   San is used after a personal name having the meaning of Mr., Mrs. and Miss. **San** differs from English terms of respect as it can be used after a first name as well as a last name. A person named Kazuo Tanaka can be called **Tanaka-san** or **Kazuo-san.**

5. **(Noun 1) wa (Noun 2) desu.**

   The particle **wa** indicates the subject of the sentence. **Wa** follows noun 1 indicating that it is the topic under discussion. Noun 2 is then identified and the phrase is concluded with **desu.**

   eg. **Watashi wa Yamamoto desu.**

         N-1   N-2

   – My name is Yamamoto.

Kochira wa Yamamoto-san desu.

   N-1   N-2

− This is Mr. Yamamoto.

Desu shows that the sentence is a statement in the present tense. It roughly corresponds to the English verb *to be* and can mean *it is, I am,* or *they are* etc. depending on the context.

6. **(Noun 1) wa (Noun 2) desu ka.**

   The particle **ka** added at the end of a sentence converts it into a question. Any statement can be made into a question by adding **ka** at the end of sentence. The word order does not change as it does in English.

   eg. (affirmative) **Yamamoto-san wa gishi desu.**

                − Mr. Yamamoto is an engineer.

   (question) **Yamamoto-san wa gishi desu ka.**

                − Is Mr. Yamamoto an engineer?

7. **Tōkyō Denki no gishi desu. Nihon Ginkō no Tanaka desu.**

   The possessive particle **no** indicates ownership or attribution and comes after the noun it modifies, like **'s** in English. Here it shows that Mr.Tanaka belongs to or works for Nihon Ginkō. Japanese individuals state their company and position when being introduced.

NIKA

Lesson 2   **Nanji desu ka** (What time is it?)

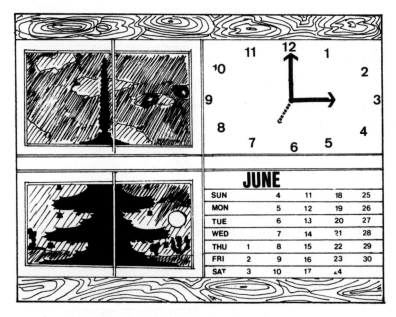

Mr. Tanaka talks with his secretary about making an international call to Mr. Smith in New York.

Tanaka: **Ima nanji desu ka.**

Hisho: **Jūichi-ji desu.**

Tanaka: **Nyūyōku shiten no Sumisu-san ni denwa shimasu ka.**

Hisho: **Iie, Ima Nyūyōku wa yoru desu. Kaisha wa asa ku-ji kara desu.**

Tanaka: **Nyūyōku wa ima nanji desu ka.**

Hisho: **Tōkyō wa gozen jūichi-ji desu kara, Nyūyōku wa gogo jū-ji goro desu.**

Tanaka: **Aa, sō desu ka.**

Hisho:	Konban denwa shimasu.
Tanaka:	Nanji goro denwa shimasu ka.
Hisho:	Yoru jūichi-ji goro denwa shimasu.

Translation

Tanaka:	What time is it now?
Secretary:	It's 11:00.
Tanaka:	Are you going to call Mr. Smith at the New York Branch?
Secretary:	No, I'm not. Now, it's night in New York. His company is open from 9:00 a.m.
Tanaka:	What time is it now in New York?
Secretary:	It's 11:00 in the morning here, so it's about 10:00 at night there.
Tanaka:	Oh, I see.
Secretary:	I'll call him tonight.
Tanaka:	About what time are you going to call him tonight?
Secretary:	I'll call him at about 11:00.

Vocabulary

hisho	secretary
ima	now
nanji	what time
nanji desu ka	what time is it?
jūichi	eleven
ji	o'clock

7

2

nyūyōku	New York
shiten	branch office
Sumisu-san	Mr. Smith
ni denwa shimasu	call, telephone (someone)
iie	no
yoru	night
kaisha	company
asa	morning
ku-ji	nine o'clock
kara	from
gozen	a.m.
kara	because
gogo	p.m.
jū-ji	ten o'clock
goro	about
sō desu ka	I see, Is that so?
konban	tonight

Explanations

1. **Ima nanji desu ka.**

   This is the most common expression used for asking the
   time. The **nan** of **nanji** means *what* and **ji** means *o'clock*.
   Nan can be used to form various compounds.

   eg. **Nan-yōbi** – Which day of the week?

        Nan-gatsu – Which month?

   Days of the week:

   nichi-yōbi – Sunday   **getsu-yōbi** – Monday

ka-yōbi – Tuesday	**sui-yōbi** – Wednesday
moku-yōbi – Thursday	**kin-yōbi** – Friday
do-yōbi – Saturday	

Months:

ichi-gatsu – January	**ni-gatsu** – February
san-gatsu – March	**shi-gatsu** – April
go-gatsu – May	**roku-gatsu** – June
shichi-gatsu – July	**hachi-gatsu** – August
ku-gatsu – September	**jū-gatsu** – October
jūichi-gatsu	**jūni-gatsu**
– November	– December

2. **Jūichi-ji desu.**

Jūichi (eleven) and **ji** combine to mean *eleven o'clock*.
The hours of the day are read in the following way.

1 – **ichi-ji**	7 – **shichi-ji**
2 – **ni-ji**	8 – **hachi-ji**
3 – **san-ji**	9 – **ku-ji**
4 – **yo-ji**	10 – **jū-ji**
5 – **go-ji**	11 – **jūichi-ji**
6 – **roku-ji**	12 – **jūni-ji**

Memorize the numbers from 0 to 20.

0 – **zero**	5 – **go**
1 – **ichi**	6 – **roku**
2 – **ni**	7 – **shichi/nana**
3 – **san**	8 – **hachi**
4 – **shi/yon**	9 – **kū/kyū**

2

10 – jū	15 – jūgo
11 – jūichi	16 – jūroku
12 – jūni	17 – jūshichi/jūnana
13 – jūsan	18 – jūhachi
14 – jūshi/jūyon	19 – jūku/jūkyū
	20 – nijū

Memorize the numbers from 20 to 100.

20 – nijū	70 – shichijū/nanajū
30 – sanjū	80 – hachijū
40 – yonjū	90 – kyūjū
50 – gojū	100 – hyaku
60 – rokujū	

Intermediate numbers are made by adding to the above numbers, the numbers from 1 to 9.

3. **Ku-ji kara desu.**

This phrase means *it is open from 9:00,* the word *open* is omitted. When the verb is understood, only the key word **kara,** followed by **desu** is often used.

SANKA

Lesson 3   **Ikura desu ka** (How much is it?)

Mr. Tanaka goes shopping at a camera store.

Tenin: Irasshaimase.

Tanaka: Kamera o misete kudasai.

Tenin: Dore desu ka.

Tanaka: Chiisai kamera desu.

Tenin: Kore desu ka. Dōzo.

Tanaka: Kore wa Doitsu no kamera desu ka.

Tenin: Iie, chigaimasu. Nihon no desu.

Tanaka: Kore wa ikura desu ka.

Tenin: Yonman-gosen-en desu.

Tanaka: Motto yasui no arimasu ka.

Tenin:	**Hai, chotto matte kudasai. Kore wa ikaga desu ka.**
Tanaka:	**Kore wa karui desu ne. Ikura desu ka.**
Tenin:	**Sanman-nisen-en desu.**
Tanaka:	**Jā, kore o kudasai. Sorekara fuirumu o futatsu kudasai.**
Tenin:	**Maido arigatō gozaimasu.**

Translation

Store clerk:	May I help you?
Tanaka:	Would you show me a camera, please?
Store clerk:	Which one, sir?
Tanaka:	That small camera.
Store clerk:	This one? Here you are.
Tanaka:	Is it a German camera?
Store clerk:	No, it isn't. It's Japanese.
Tanaka:	How much is it?
Store clerk:	It's ¥45,000.
Tanaka:	Do you have a cheaper one?
Store clerk:	Certainly. Wait a moment, please. How do you like this one?
Tanaka:	It's light, isn't it? How much is it?
Store clerk:	It's ¥32,000.
Tanaka:	Well then, I'll take it. And please give me two rolls of film.
Store clerk:	Thank you very much.

Vocabulary

tenin	store clerk
irasshaimase	Come in. Welcome.
kamera	camera
o	object marker, particle
misete kudasai	please show me
misemasu	show
dore	which
chiisai	small
kore	this
Doitsu	Germany
Doitsu no	German
chigaimasu	that's wrong
Nihon	Japan
Nihon no	Japanese
ikura	how much
ikura desu ka	how much is it?
yonman	40,000
gosen	5,000
yonman-gosen	45,000
en	yen
yasui	cheap
motto yasui	cheaper
arimasu ka	is there? do you have?
chotto	a moment
matte kudasai	please wait
ikaga desu ka	how do you like

3

karui	light
ne	isn't it?
sanman	30,000
nisen	2,000
sanmen-nisen	32,000
jā	well then
kudasai	please give me
sorekara	and
fuirumu	film
futatsu	two
maido	every time
arigatō gozaimasu	thank you very much

Explanations

1. **Irasshaimase**

   This is a greeting used by a sales clerk speaking to a customer.

2. **Kore, sore**

   English has only *this* and *that* but Japanese has three separate indicators: **kore, sore, are.**

   Kore indicates something near the speaker.

   Sore indicates something near the person spoken to.

   Are indicates something not near either person.

3. **Chigaimasu.**

   Chigaimasu literally means *that's wrong.* This phrase is very often used to mean *no, it isn't* in daily conversation.

14

4. Numbers from 100 to 100,000,000.

100 − **hyaku**	4,000 − **yonsen**
200 − **nihyaku**	5,000 − **gosen**
300 − **sanbyaku**	6,000 − **rokusen**
400 − **yonhyaku**	7,000 − **nanasen**
500 − **gohyaku**	8,000 − **hassen**
600 − **roppyaku**	9,000 − **kyūsen**
700 − **nanahyaku**	10,000 − **ichiman**
800 − **happyaku**	100,000 − **jūman**
900 − **kyūhyaku**	1,000,000 − **hyakuman**
1000 − **sen**	10,000,000 − **senman**
2,000 − **nisen**	100,000,000 − **ichioku**
3,000 − **sanzen**	

5. **Kore wa karui desu ne.**

   This means *It is light, isn't it?* The particle **ne** comes at the end of a sentence or phrase and, like *you see?* or *isn't it?* in English, seeks the confirmation and agreement of the other person.

6. **Kore o kudasai.**

   Kudasai *please give me* follows the object (a noun) with object marker **o.**

   eg. **Kamera o kudasai.** − Please give me that camera.

7. **Futatsu**

   In Japanese there are two numerical systems, the **hitotsu, futatsu** system and the abstract **ichi, ni** system. Counting things can be done in two ways and **ichi, ni** system is combined with a counter.

3

Single units of most objects are counted in the following way:

1 – hitotsu	6 – muttsu
2 – futatsu	7 – nanatsu
3 – mittsu	8 – yattsu
4 – yottsu	9 – kokonotsu
5 – itsutsu	10 – tō

The **hitotsu, futatsu** numbering system only goes as far as ten, after which the **ichi, ni** numbering system is used.

YONKA

Lesson 4   **Doko desu ka** (Where is it?)

Mr. Brown is asking a woman how to get to the post office.

Brown: Sumimasen. Kono chikaku ni yūbinkyoku ga arimasu ka.

Woman: Ee, arimasu yo.

Brown: Doko ni arimasu ka.

Woman: Asoko ni ginkō ga arimasu ne. Yūbinkyoku wa ano ginkō no tonari desu.

Brown: Ginkō no ushiro ni shiroi tatemono ga arimasu ne. Are wa nan desu ka.

Woman: Are wa hoteru desu.

Brown: Hoteru ni kōshū-denwa ga arimasu ka.

Woman: Ee, robii ni arimasu.

4

Brown:	Tokorode, yūbinkyoku wa nanji made desu ka.
Woman:	Kyō wa do-yōbi desu kara, yūbinkyoku wa jūni-ji made desu.
Brown:	Dōmo arigatō.
Woman:	Dō itashimashite.

Translation

Brown:	Excuse me. Is there a post office near here?
Woman:	Yes, there is.
Brown:	Where is it?
Woman:	See that bank over there? The post office is next to that bank.
Brown:	There is a white building behind the bank. What is that?
Woman:	That is a hotel.
Brown:	Is there a public telephone in the hotel?
Woman:	Yes, there is a public telephone in the lobby.
Brown:	By the way, what time does the post office close?
Woman:	Today is Saturday, so the post office closes at 12:00 noon.
Brown:	Thank you.
Woman:	You're welcome.

Vocabulary

sumimasen	excuse me

18

kono chikaku	near here
yūbinkyoku	post office
arimasu ka	is there
doko	where
asoko	over there
ginkō	bank
ano	that
tonari	next to
ushiro	behind
shiroi	white
tatemono	building
are	that
nan	what
hoteru	hotel
kōshū-denwa	public telephone
robii	lobby
tokorode	by the way
made	until
nanji made	until what time
kyō	today
do-yōbi	Saturday
kara	because, so
jūni-ji	12:00
dō itashimashite	you're welcome

4

Explanations

1. **Sumimasen**

   Sumimasen, *excuse me,* perfaces a request, such as asking a stranger for information. It can also mean *thank you* or *I'm sorry.*

2. **Arimasu**

   Arimasu is used for inanimate things (books, buildings, tree, etc.) to express *being.*

3. Particle **ni.**

   Existence in a place is indicated by the particle **ni.**

   eg. **Kono chikaku ni yūbinkyoku ga arimasu.**

   Asoko ni ginkō ga arimasu.

   Hoteru ni kōshū-denwa ga arimasu.

4. **Ee, arimasu yo.**

   The particle **yo** is added to the end of a sentence to call attention to information the speaker thinks the other person does not know.

5. **Relative positions.**

	ue (on, over, above, on top of)	
	shita (under, below)	
	mae (in front of)	
Noun no	**ushiro** (behind, at the back of)	**ni arimasu**
	naka (in, inside)	
	hidari (to the left of)	
	migi (to the right of)	

GOKA

Lesson 5   **Kazoku** (Family)

Mr. Tanaka was invited to a party at Michiko's house.

Tanaka: Asoko ni otoko no hito ga imasu ne.

Michiko: Doko ni imasu ka?

Tanaka: Kuruma no mae ni imasu.

Michiko: Aa, sō desu ne.

Tanaka: Ano hito wa dare desu ka.

Michiko: Yamamoto-san no otō-san desu.

Tanaka: Onna no hito mo imasu ne.

Michiko: Ee, Yamamoto-san no okā-san desu.

Tanaka: Ano hito tachi wa Yamamoto-san no go-ryōshin desu ka.

Michiko: Anata no oku-san wa doko ni imasu ka.

5

Tanaka:	Watashi no kanai wa ima ni imasu. Michiko-san no otō-san wa?
Michiko:	Chichi wa niwa ni imasu.
Tanaka:	Okā-san wa doko ni imasu ka.
Michiko:	Haha wa daidokoro ni imasu.
Tanaka:	Aa, are wa anata no onē-san desu ka.
Michiko:	Ee, are wa ane desu.

Translation

Tanaka:	There is a man over there.
Michiko:	Where?
Tanaka:	In front of the car.
Michiko:	Oh, yes, there is.
Tanaka:	Who is he?
Michiko:	He is Mr. Yamamoto's father.
Tanaka:	There is a woman, too.
Michiko:	Yes, she is Mr. Yamamoto's mother.
Tanaka:	They are Mr. Yamamoto's parents, aren't they?
Michiko:	Where is your wife?
Tanaka:	My wife is in the living room. Where is your father?
Michiko:	My father is in the garden.
Tanaka:	Where is your mother?
Michiko:	My mother is in the kitchen.
Tanaka:	Oh, is that your elder sister?
Michiko:	Yes, that is my elder sister.

5

Vocabulary

Michiko	girl's first name
otoko	man
hito	person
imasu	there is
doko	where
kuruma	car
mae	in front of
ano hito	that person
dare	who
dare desu ka	who is that?
otō-san/chichi	father
onna no hito	woman
mo	too
okā-san/haha	mother
ano hito tachi	those people
ryōshin/goryoshin	parents
anata	you
anata no	your
oku-san/kanai	wife
ima	living room
niwa	garden
daidokoro	kitchen
onē-san/ane	elder sister

5

Explanations

1. **Asoko.**

   Asoko is used to refer to a place which is not close to either the speaker or the person spoken to.

2. **Imasu.**

   The verb **imasu** means *being* and is used for animate things, people, animals, insects etc.

3. **Doko ni imasu ka.**

   Doko means *where.* (Noun) **wa doko ni imasu ka** is used to ask the location of living things.

4. **-tachi.**

   Tachi is a plural suffix for people and is added to names and nouns indicating people.

   e.g. **watashi** (I) − **watashitachi** (we)

   anata (you) − **anatatachi** (you)

   otoko ni hito (man) −**otoko no hitotachi** (men)

5. **Family terms.**

   The following is a list of names for family members. When talking about their own family members to other persons, Japanese use plain terms. When talking about other's families, they use polite terms.

	Related to the speaker	Related to others
both parents	ryōshin	goryōshin
father	chichi	otō-san
mother	haha	okā-san
husband	shujin	goshujin
wife	kanai	oku-san
elder brother	ani	onii-san
younger brother	otōto	otōto-san
elder sister	ane	onē-san
younger sister	imōto	imōto-san

ROKKA

Lesson 6   **Nanji ni okimasu ka**

(At what time do you rise?)

Mr. Tanaka and Miss Suzuki meet in the street and talk while walking to the station.

Tanaka:	**Ohayōgozaimasu.**
Suzuki:	**Ohayōgozaimasu. Kyō wa ii tenki desu ne.**
Tanaka:	**Sō desu ne.**
Suzuki:	**Tanaka-san wa maiasa nanji ni okimasu ka.**
Tanaka:	**Roku-ji ni okimasu.**
Suzuki:	**Hayai desu ne. Watashi wa shichi-ji goro okimasu.**
	Nanji goro nemasu ka.
Tanaka:	**Jūichi-ji han goro nemasu.**

Suzuki:	Kaisha wa nanji ni hajimarimasu ka.
Tanaka:	Ku-ji ni hajimarimasu.
Suzuki:	Nanji ni owarimasu ka.
Tanaka:	Go-ji goro owarimasu.
Suzuki:	Mainichi kaisha e ikimasu ka.
Tanaka:	Ee.
Suzuki:	Do-yōbi ni mo ikimasu ka.
Tanaka:	Ee, do-yōbi wa jūni-ji made desu.
Suzuki:	Watashi wa do-yōbi wa kaisha e ikimasen. Yasumi desu.

Translation

Tanaka:	Good morning.
Suzuki:	Good morning, It's a fine day today, isn't it?
Tanaka:	Yes, it is.
Suzuki:	What time do you get up every morning?
Tanaka:	I get up at six.
Suzuki:	That's early. I get up at about seven. What time do you go to bed?
Tanaka:	At about 11:30.
Suzuki:	What time does your office start?
Tanaka:	At nine.
Suzuki:	What time does it finish?
Tanaka:	It finishes at about five.
Suzuki:	Do you go to the office every day?
Tanaka:	Yes, I do.
Suzuki:	On Saturdays, too?

6

Tanaka:	Yes, the office opens until 12 o'clock on Saturdays.
Suzuki:	I don't go to the office on Saturdays. Saturdays are holidays.

Vocabulary

ohayōgozaimasu	good morning
kyō	today
ii	good/fine
tenki	weather
maiasa	every morning
ni	at, on
ku-ji ni	at 9 o'clock
do-yōbi ni	on Saturday
okimasu	get up
roku-ji	6 o'clock
hayai	early
shichi-ji	7 o'clock
goro	about
nemasu	go to bed
jūichi-ji han	11:30
han	half, thirty minutes
kaisha	office, company
hajimarimasu	start
ku-ji	9 o'clock
owarimasu	finish
go-ji	5 o'clock

6

mainichi	every day
e ikimasu	go to
ni mo	too
jūni-ji	12 o'clock
ikimasen	negative form of **ikamasu**
yasumi	break, holiday

Explanations

1. **Verb -masu form.**

   In ordinary polite speech, the present affirmative form of all verbs end with **masu**: eg. **okimasu, nemasu, hajimarimasu, owarimasu, ikimasu.** **V-masu** expresses actions or events which regularly or repeatedly take place, like habitual actions, or which will take place in the future. There is no future tense as such in Japanese.

2. **Ni**

   The particle **ni** indicates the time of action and means *at, on, in.*

   eg. **go-ji ni** − at 5 o'clock   **do-yōbi ni** − on Saturday
   gogo ni − in the afternoon

3. **Goro.**

   Goro is used to show approximate time and it doesn't connect the particle **ni.**

   eg. **yo-ji ni** − at four o'clock   **yo-ji goro** − at about four o'clock

6

4. **Kaisha e ikimasu.**

   E is the particle indicating direction. Japanese particles resemble English prepositions in the way they connect words, but they always come after nouns. The role of preposition *to* in English is played by the particle **e** in Japanese.

5. **Do-yōbi ni mo ikimasu ka.**

   The particle **mo** means *too, also* and it is added after the particle **ni** to indicate the time of action.

NANAKA

Lesson 7   **Doko e ikimasu ka** (Where are you going?)

Mr. Tanaka meets Mr. Yamamoto in the street. Mr. Yamamoto looks as if he is going on a trip.

Tanaka: **Yamamoto-san, doko e ikimasu ka.**

Yamamoto: **Ōsaka no shisha e ikimasu.**

Tanaka: **Hitori de ikimasu ka.**

Yamamoto: **Iie, kaisha no hito to ikimasu.**

Tanaka: **Hikōki de ikimasu ka.**

Yamamoto: **Iie, Shinkansen de ikimasu.**

Tanaka: **Donogurai kakarimasu ka.**

Yamamoto: **Tōkyō kara Ōsaka made san-jikan gurai kakarimasu.**

Tanaka: **Donogurai achira ni imasu ka.**

7

Yamamoto:	Itsuka kan imasu.
Tanaka:	Kyōto e mo ikimasu ka.
Yamamoto:	Iie, Kyōto e wa ikimasen. Mainichi kaigi ga arimasu kara totemo isogashii desu.
Tanaka:	Itsu Tōkyō e kaerimasu ka.
Yamamoto:	Hatsuka ni kaerimasu.

Translation

Tanaka:	Where are you going?
Yamamoto:	I'm going to our branch office in Osaka.
Tanaka:	Are you going alone?
Yamamoto:	No, I'm going with a person from the company.
Tanaka:	Are you going by airplane?
Yamamoto:	No, we're going by Shinkansen.
Tanaka:	How long does it take by Shinkansen?
Yamamoto:	It takes about three hours from Tokyo to Osaka.
Tanaka:	How long are you going to stay there?
Yamamoto:	For five days.
Tanaka:	Are you going to Kyoto, too?
Yamamoto:	No, we're not going to Kyoto. We'll have meetings every day so we'll be busy.
Tanaka:	When are you coming back to Tokyo?
Yamamoto:	We're returning on 20th.

Vocabulary

Ōsaka	name of the city
shisha	branch office
hitori de	alone
to	with
hikōki	airplane
de	by
Shinkansen	bullet train
donogurai	how long
kakarimasu	take (in time)
kara − made	from − to
san-jikan	three hours
jikan	hour
achira	there
imasu	stay
itsuka	five days
kan	for (a period of)
Kyōto	name of the city
mo	too
mainichi	every day
kaigi	meeting
arimasu	there is
kara	because, so
totemo	very
isogashii	busy
itsu	when
kaerimasu	return

7

hatsuka	20th
ni	on

Explanations

1. **Hitori de.**

   Words expressing *Number of people* take the particle **de.**

   eg.**hitori de** — alone   **futari de** — two of us

   People are counted in the following way.

hitori — 1 person	**roku-nin** — 6 people
futari — 2 people	**shichi-nin** — 7 people
san-nin — 3 people	**hachi-nin** — 8 people
yo-nin — 4 people	**kyū-nin** — 9 people
go-nin — 5 people	**jū-nin** — 10 people

   Above ten - **jū-nin** is added to the set of numbers.

2. **Hikōki de ikimasu.**

   The particle **de** follows the noun to express the mode of transportation.

   eg. **basu de** — by bus   **kuruma de** — by car

   takushii de — by taxi

3. **Donogurai.**

   An approximate time period is expressed by the suffix - **gurai.**

   eg. **san-jikan gurai** — about three hours

   itsuka gurai — about five days

Donogurai is used to ask how long it takes.

eg. **Donogurai kakarimasu ka** – How long does it take?

4. **Days of the month.**

1st – **tsuitachi**	17th – **jūshichi-nich**
2nd – **futsuka**	18th – **jūhachi-nichi**
3rd – **mikka**	19th – **jūku-nich**
4th – **yokka**	20th – **hatsuka**
5th – **itsuka**	21st – **nijūichi-nich**
6th – **muika**	22nd – **nijūni-nichi**
7th – **nanoka**	23rd – **nijūsan-nichi**
8th – **yōka**	24th – **nijūyokka**
9th – **kokonoka**	25th – **nijūgo-nichi**
10th – **tōka**	26th – **nijūroku-nichi**
11th – **jūichi-nichi**	27th – **nijūshichi-nichi**
12th – **jūni-nichi**	28th – **nijūhachi-nichi**
13th – **jūsan-nichi**	29th – **nijūku-nichi**
14th – **jūyokka**	30th – **sanjū-nichi**
15th – **jūgo-nichi**	31st – **sanjūichi-nichi**
16th – **jūroku-nichi**	

5. **Kyōto e wa ikimasen.**

In negative replies, the particle **wa** is used.

eg. **Kyōto e mo ikimasu ka. Iie Kyōto e wa ikimasen.**

HAKKA

Lesson 8 Nani o shimashita ka (What did you do?)

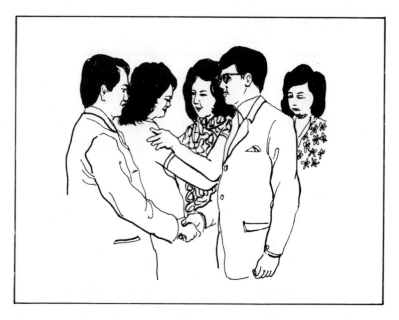

Two acquaintances are talking on a Monday morning.

A: **Kinō wa yoku ame ga furimashita ne.**

B: **Sō desu ne. Ichinichi-jū furimashita ne.**

A: **Doko ka e ikimashita ka.**

B: **Iie, doko e mo ikimasendeshita. Uchi de rajio o kikimashita.**

   Anata wa kinō nani o shimashita ka.

A: **Hon o yomimashita, sorekara terebi o mimashita.**

B: **Donna hon o yomimashita ka.**

A: **Shōsetsu desu.**

B: **Watashi wa gakusei no toki yoku hon o yomimashita ga ima wa amari yomimasen.**

A: Sō desu ka. Supōtsu mo shimashita ka.

B: Ee, shimashita yo. Yakyū to tenisu to suiē o shimashita.

A: Iroiro na supōtsu o shimashita ne.

B: Ee, demo benkyō wa amari shimasendeshita.

Translation

A: It rained a lot yesterday, didn't it?

B: Yes, it did. It rained all day.

A: Did you go anywhere?

B: No, I didn't. I listened to the radio at home. What did you do yesterday?

A: I read a book and watched TV.

B: What kind of book did you read?

A: A novel.

B: I used to read a lot when I was a student but I don't read much now.

A: I see. Did you take part in sports?

B: Yes, I did. I played baseball, tennis and swam.

A: You were quite active, weren't you?

B: Yes, but I didn't do much studying.

Vocabulary

kinō	yesterday
yoku	a lot
ame	rain (noun)

8

furimashita	fell (**furimasu** – fall-rain, snow, hail)
ichinichi-jū	all day
doko ka	anywhere
ikimashita	went (**ikimasu** – go)
doko e mo	nowhere
ikimasendenshita	did not go
uchi de	at home
rajio	radio
o	particle, object marker
kikimashita	listened to (**kikimasu** – listen)
nani	what
shimashita	did (**shimasu** – do)
hon	book
yomimashita	read (**yomimasu** – read)
sorekara	and then
terebi	TV
mimashita	watched (**mimasu** – watch)
donna	what kind
shōsetsu	novel
gakusei	student
no toki	when
yoku ... -mashita	used to
ga	but
amari	not too much
yomimasen	do not read
supōtsu	sports
yakyū	baseball

tenisu	tennis
to	and
suiei	swimming
iroiro na	various
demo	but
benkyō	studying

Explanations

1. **Past tense of verbs; V-mashita.**

   The past tense of **-masu** is **-mashita**. Memorize the
   following verbs and their present and past tense forms.

(Present tense)

	(aff.)	(neg.)
is	**desu**	**dewa arimasen**
be	**arimasu**	**arimasen**
be	**imasu**	**imasen**
show	**misemasu**	**misemasen**
wait	**machimasu**	**machimasen**
get up	**okimasu**	**okimasen**
go to bed	**nemasu**	**nemasen**
begin	**hajimarimasu**	**hajimarimasen**
finish	**owarimasu**	**owarimasen**
go	**ikimasu**	**ikimasen**
take	**kakarimasu**	**kakarimasen**
return	**kaerimasu**	**kaerimasen**
fall	**furimasu**	**furimasen**

8

listen	kikimasu	kikimasen
do	shimasu	shimasen
read	yomimasu	yomimasen
watch	mimasu	mimasen

(Past tense)

	(aff.)	(neg.)
is	deshita	dewa arimasendenshita
be	arimashita	arimasendeshita
be	imashita	imasendenshita
show	misemashita	misemasendeshita
wait	machimashita	machimasendeshita
get up	okimashita	okimasendeshita
go to bed	nemashita	nemasendeshita
begin	hajimarimashita	hajimarimasendeshita
finish	owarimashita	owarimasendeshita
go	ikimashita	ikimasendeshita
take	kakarimashita	kakarimasendeshita
return	kaerimashita	kaerimasendeshita
fall	furimashita	furimasendeshita
listen	kikimashita	kikimasendeshita
do	shimashita	shimasendeshita
read	yomimashita	yomimasendeshita
watch	mimashita	mimasendeshita

2. **Doko ka, doko e mo.**

When interrogative nouns are immediately followed by

ka or, **mo,** they lose their interrogative meaning.

e.g. **doko** − where **doko ka** − anywhere **doko e mo** −
nowhere

Doko e ikimashita ka. − Where did you go?

Doko ka e ikimashita ka. − Did you go anywhere?

Iie, doko e mo ikimasendeshita. − No, I didn't go
anywhere.

3. **(Person) + wa + (Noun) + O-verb.**

A transitive verb usually follows **o** which indicates a
direct object. **O** is used with verbs, such as *read, do,
drink, eat* and many others.

4. **Particle *de*.**

De is used to indicate the place where an action is
performed.

eg. **Uchi de** − at home **Kaisha de** − at our company

KYŪKA

Lesson 9   **Oishii okashi** (Delicious cakes)

Michiko is offering Mr. Brown a cup of tea.

Michiko:	Ocha o dōzo.
Brown:	Arigatō gozaimasu.
Michiko:	Okashi wa ikaga desu ka.
Brown:	Hai, itadakimasu. Kireina okashi desu ne. Nihon no okashi desu ka.
Michiko:	Ee, sō desu. Dōzo meshiagatte kudasai.
Brown:	Totemo oishii desu.
Michiko:	Buraun-san no o-kuni wa dochira desu ka.
Brown:	Igirisu desu. Watashi no uchi wa Rondon ni arimasu.
Michiko:	Rondon wa atsui desu ka.

Brown:	Iie, amari atsuku nai desu. Suzushii desu.
	Rondon wa furui machi desu.
Michiko:	Yūmeina hakubutsukan ga arimasu ne.
Brown:	Anata no machi wa donna machi desu ka.
Michiko:	Chiisai machi desu ga shizukana tokoro desu.
	Aa, ocha o mō ippai ikaga desu ka.
Brown:	Iie, mō kekkō desu.

Translation

Michiko:	Please have some tea.
Brown:	Thank you.
Michiko:	Will you have a cake?
Brown:	Yes, I'd love one. What pretty cakes! Are they Japanese cakes?
Michiko:	Yes, they are. Please help yourself.
Brown:	They are delicious.
Michiko:	Where are you from?
Brown:	I'm from England and my house is in London.
Michiko:	Is it hot in London?
Brown:	No, it's not so hot, it's cool. London is an old city.
Michiko:	There is a famous museum there, isn't there?
Brown:	Yes. What kind of town is your home town?
Michiko:	It's a small town but it's quite. Oh, will you have another cup of tea?
Brown:	No, thank you. That is enough.

9

Vocabulary

ocha	tea
dōzo	please
okashi	cake
ikaga	how
ikaga desu ka	How about ....?
itadakimasu	eat (polite form of **tabemasu**)
kirei (na)	pretty, clean
meshiagatte kudasai	please eat (polite form of **tabete kudasai**)
totemo	very
oishii	delicious
o-kuni	country (polite form of **kuni**)
dochira	where (polite form of **doko**)
Igirisu	England
uchi	house
Rondon	London
atsui	hot
atsuku nai	not hot
suzushii	cool
furui	old
machi	town, city
yūmei (na)	famous
hakubutsukan	museum
donna	what kind of
chiisai	small
shizuka (na)	quite

9

tokoro	place
mō	more, another
ippai	1 cupful
mō kekkō desu	no thank you, that was enough

Explanations

1. **Japanese adjectives.**

   Japanese adjectives can either modify nouns by immediately preceding them or act as predicates. Unlike English adjectives, Japanese adjectivs are inflected so that their endings show present or past, affirmative or negative. There are two kinds of adjectives: **-i** adjectives and **-na** adjectives. The adjectives end with **-na** when they come before nouns and are called **-na** adjectives while **oishii, furui** ect. are called **-i** adjectives.

2. **Negative form of adjectives.**

   An **-i** adjective plus **desu,** form may be converted into a *negative* by changing **i** to **ku** with **nai desu.**

   eg. oishii desu − oishiku nai desu

       atsui desu − atsuku nai desu

   A **-na** adjective plus **desu** form may be converted into a *negative* by replacing **desu** with **dewa arimasen.**

   Memorize the following **-i** adjectives. All the adjectives behave in the same way with the exception of **ii,** *good.*

45

9

	(affirmative)	(negative)	(modifying noun)
delicious	oishii	oishiku nai	oishii
hot	atsui	atsuku nai	atsui
cool	suzushii	suzushiku nai	suzushii
old	furui	furuku nai	furui
small	chiisai	chiisaku nai	chiisai
big	ōkii	ōkiku nai	ōkii
new	atarashii	atarashiku nai	atarashii
expensive	takai	takaku nai	takai
cheap	yasui	yasuku nai	yasui
interesting	omoshiroi	omoshiroku nai	omoshiroi
easy	yasashii	yasashiku nai	yasashii
difficult	muzukashii	muzukashiku nai	muzukashii
good	ii	yoku nai	ii

Memorize the following **-na** adjectives.

	(affirmative)	(negative)	(modifying noun)
pretty	**kirei**	**kirei dewa arimasen**	**kireina**
famous	**yūmei**	**yūmei dewa arimasen**	**yūmeina**
quiet	**shizuka**	**shizuka dewa arimasen**	**shizukana**
well	**genki**	**genki dewa arimasen**	**genkina**
kind	**shinsetsu**	**shinsetsu dewa arimasen**	**shinsetsuna**
convenient	**benri**	**benri dewa arimasen**	**benrina**

3. **Ikaga desu ka.**

A polite way of saying **dō desu ka.** *How is it?* This phrase is often used when offering things like food and drink, meaning *Would you like one?*

4. **Itadakimasu.**

A polite word for **tabemasu,** *I eat.* It is used when taking something that is offered, implying both acceptance and gratitude.

Japanese mealtime conventions:

Before eating:

Itadakimasu.   *I gratefully partake.*

9

After eating:

Gochisōsama. *Thank you for a lovely meal.*

5. **Iie, mō kekkō desu.**

This is a polite way of refusing something offered.

JUKKA

Lesson 10   **Shōtai** (An invitation)

Mr. Hayashi and Michiko are making a date to go to the movies.

Michiko: **Eiga no kippu ga ni-mai arimasu. Konban issho ni ikimasen ka.**

Hayashi: **Zannen desu ga konban hachi-ji ni kūkō e ikimasu.**

Michiko: **Ryokō desu ka.**

Hayashi: **Iie, tomodachi ga Honkon kara kimasu.**

Michiko: **Tomodachi wa itsu made Nihon ni imasu ka.**

Hayashi: **Raishū no moku-yōbi made imasu.**

Michiko: **Sō desu ka.**

Hayashi: **Ashita no yoru issho ni shokuji o shimasen ka.**

10

Michiko:	Ii desu ne.
Hayashi:	Shichi-ji han ni ABC biru no mae de aimashō ka.
Michiko:	Hai, wakarimashita. Jā, ashita.

Translation

Michiko:	I have two tickets for the movies. Would you like to go with me tonight?
Hayashi:	I'm sorry, but I'm going to the airport at 8 o'clock tonight.
Michiko:	Are you going on a trip?
Hayashi:	No, my friend is coming from Hong Kong.
Michiko:	How long is your friend staying in Japan?
Hayashi:	He will be in Japan until next Thursday.
Michiko:	I see.
Hayashi:	Would you like to have dinner with us tomorrow?
Michiko:	I'd love to.
Hayashi:	Shall we meet in front of ABC building at 7:30 tomorrow?
Michiko:	Sure, that's fine. Well, see you tomorrow.

Vocabulary

eiga	movies
kippu	ticket
ni-mai	two

mai	counter for paper
arimasu	I have
konban	tonight
issho ni	together
ikimasen ka	won't you go
zannen	unfortunately
kūkō	airport
e ikimasu	go to
ryokō	trip
tomodachi	friend
Honkon	Hong Kong
kara	from
kimasu	come
itsu made	until when
imasu	stay
raishū	next week
moku-yōbi	Thursday
raishū no moku-yōbi	next Thursday
ashita	tomorrow
yoru	night, evening
ashita no yoru	tomorrow night
shokuji o shimasu	have a meal
shokuji o shimasen ka	would you like to have a meal with me?
ii	good, nice
shichi-ji han	7:30

10

biru	building
no mae	in front of
aimasu	meet
aimashō	let's meet
aimashō ka	shall we meet?
wakarimashita	sure, certainly
jā	well

Explanations

1. **Verb - *masen ka.***

   -masen ka is used for inviting a person to do something with you.

   eg. **issho ni ikimasen ka** − Would you like to go with me?

   shokuji o shimasen ka − Would you like to have a meal with me?

2. **Replies to the above.**

   The following English equivalents give an idea of the appropriate replies.

   Acceptance: 1. **Hai, zehi.** − I'd love to.

   2. **Hai,** verb **-mashō.** − Yes, let's ....

   3. **Hai,** verb **-masu.** − O.K.

   4. **Hai, onegaishimasu.** − Yes, please.

   Refusal: 5. **Zannen desu ga, tsugō ga warui desu.**

   − I'm sorry, I'm afraid I have another engagement

   6. **Iie, kekkō desu.** − No, thank you.

3. **Relative time.**

   (1) Day

   ototoi – day before   **kinō** – yesterday
            yesterday
   kyō – today   **ashita** – tomorrow
   asatte – day after
            tomorrow

   (2) Morning

   ototoi no asa – morning   **kinō no asa** – yesterday
            before last   morning
   kesa – this morning   **ashita no asa** – tomorrow
                                           morning
   asatte no asa – morning of the day after tomorrow

   (3) Evening

   ototoi no yoru – night   **kinō no yoru yūbe** -- last night
            before last
   konban – tonight   **ashita no yoru** – tomorrow
                                           night

   (4) Week

   senshū – last week   **konshū** – this week
   raishū – next week   **saraishū** – week after next

   (5) Month

   sengetsu – last month   **kongetsu** – this month
   raigetsu – next month   **saraigetsu** – month after next

INDEX OF GRAMMATICAL POINTS

The first number refers to the *Lesson* and the number in the brackets is the paragraph of the *Explanations*.

JAPANESE-ENGLISH DICTIONARY

A

aa oh! Ah!
abekku a couple (on a date), date
abunai dangerous
abura oil, fat, grease
achira there
agarimas, ageru raises up; gives
aida interval; between; while
aimashō let's meet
aimashō ka shall we meet?
aimasu meet
ainiku unfortunately
aisatsu greetings
aite the other fellow (companion; adversary)
aitsu that one over there, that fellow (chap)
ajā, ajappā well, I'll be...
aji taste
akai red
aka-chan baby
akambō baby
akarui bright, light
akemas', akeru opens; leaves empty
aki autumn, fall
amai sweet
ame rain; candy
ami net
ammari too much, overly
ana hole
anata you
anata no your
anata tachi you (plural)
anata wa? and you?
ane (my) elder sister
ani (my) elder brother
ano that (over there)
ano hito that person
ano hito tachi those people
aoi blue; green
arai rough, coarse
araimas', arau wash
aratamemas', aratameru change, alter

arawaremas', arawareru appear, show
ari ant
arigato gozaimasu thank you very much
arimasen there isn't, aren't
arimasu ka is there?, do you have?
aru a certain
arubaito a side job, a sideline
arui-wa or else, maybe
arukimas', aruku walk
asa morning
asagohan breakfast
asai shallow
asatte day after tomorrow
asatte no asa morning of the day after tomorrow
ase sweat
ashi foot; leg
ashita tomorrow
ashita no asa tomorrow morning
ashita no yoru tomorrow night
asobi fun; a game; a visit
asoko over there
atama head
atarashii new
atarimas', ataru hit; face; apply; is correct
at(a)takai warm
atemas', ateru guesses; hits; sets aside, appropriates, designates; touches; addresses
atena address
ato after(wards), later
atsui hot; thick
atsuku nai not hot
atsumarimas', atsumaru meet, assemble
atsumemas', atsumeru collect, gather
au (aimas') meet, see (a person)
awasemas', awaseru puts together, combine
azarashi seal (animal)
azukemas' azukeru entrust, checks deposit

B

-ba place
baai, bawai situation, case, circumstance
bai double
baka fool, idiot, stupid
ban guard, watch; number; evening
bangohan dinner, supper
basho place
basu bus; bath
batā butter
Beikoku America
beni rogue; lipstick
benjo toilet
benkyō studying
benri convenient, handy
bentō (box) lunch
betsu separate, special, particular
biiru beer
bin bottle; jar
biru building
bōi boy, waiter, steward, clerk
boku I, me (man speaking)
bōrupen ball point pen
bōshi hat
botan button
bozu Buddhist monk or priest
bu part, division, section
budō grapes
budō-shu wine
bumpō grammar
bun part, portion, share; state; status
bungo literary language
bunka culture
bunsho (written) sentence
buta pig
buta-niku pork
byōin hospital
byōki sick; sickness

C

cha tea
chadai a tip

chakku zipper
chanpon alternating, skipping back and forth, mixing one's drinks
chi blood
chichi (my) father; breasts; mother's milk
chigaimas' chigau is different; is wrong; isn't like that
chihō area, region, a locality
chiisai, chiisa-na little, small
chiizu cheese
chika subway; underground; basement
chikai near, close by
chika-michi short cut
chikki check, receipt, stub
chikuonki phonograph
chiri geography
chiri-gami Japanese Kleenex and toilet paper
chizu map
chō block of a city; head, chief, leader
chōdai please; I (humbly) take
chokki vest
chokusetsu direct
chō-kyori long distance
chōsa examination, investigation, inquiry
Chōsen Korea
chotto just a little; just a minute
chū middle, medium
chūgata medium-size (model)
Chūgoku China
Chūgokugo Chinese (language)
Chūgokujin Chinese (people)
chūi attention
chūshin center

D

da (des) is; it is
da ga but
dai- big
dai- (ichi) number (one)

daiben bowel movement
daidokoro kitchen
daigaku college or university
daigakusē college student
daiji important, precious
daijōbu OK, all right; safe and
  sound; no need to worry
daiku carpenter
daitai in general, on the whole,
  approximately, almost
da kara (sa) and so; therefore; that's
  why
dakimas', daku hold in one's arms,
  hug, embrace
damarimas', damaru is silent;
  shut up
damashimas', damasu to deceive
dambō heating (in a house)
dame no good, no use, won't do;
  don't!
dandan gradually
danna (san) master of the house;
  husband
dantai organization, group
dare who
dare desu ka who is that?
dare ga imasu ka who is there?
dare ka someone, anyone
dare mo everybody; nobody
dare no whose
dashi soup-stock
dashimas', dasu put out; produces;
  spends; mails; begins
da tte but, though
de (happening) at, in, on; with, by
  (means of)
is and; being, its being; with (its
  being)
deguchi exit
dekigoto happening, an accident
dekimas' dekiru can, is possible; is
  produced; is finished, ready
dekimono swelling, sore, boil,
  pimple

demas', deru goes out, comes out,
  leaves, starts
dembu buttocks, hips
de mo but, however, even so
dempō telegram
denki electricity; lights
dentō lamp, light, flashlight, tradition,
  convention
denwa telephone (call)
depāto department store
deru (demas') goes out, comes out,
  leaves, starts
desh'ta was; it was
deshō probably is, it probably is
des', da is; it is; it is a case of ...
de wa (=ja) well then; in that case;
  and so; and now
dō how, why; (in) what (way)
doa door
dochira which one
dochira ka either one of the two
dochira mo either one; neither one;
  both
Doitsu Germany
doitsu the same as
dokimas' (doku) gets out of the way
doko where
doko ka somewhere
doko mo everywhere; nowhere
doku poison
doku (dokimas') gets out of the way
donna what kind of
dōmo thank you; excuse me ever so
  much
dono which
dore which one
doro mud
dorobō thief, robber
doru dollar
dō-sh'te why; how
doyōbi Saturday
dōzo please
dōzo yoroshiku I'm glad to meet you

E

e picture
ē yes
e to (particle)
e ikimasu go to
ebi shrimp; lobster
eda branch
e-hagaki picture postcard
e-hon picture book
eiga (-kan) movie (theater)
Eigo English
Eikoku England
eisei hygiene, health, sanitation
eki railroad station
en Yen
empitsu pencil
enkai party
ensoku picnic, outing, an excursion
entotsu chimney, smokestack
erabimas', erabu chooses, selects, elects
erai great, superior
erebeta elevator

F

fū appearance, air; way, fashion, manner
fuben inconvenient, unhandy
fuchūi carelessness
fuda label, tag, card, check
fude writing brush
fudōsan real estate
fūfu husband and wife, Mr. and Mrs.
fuhei discontent, grumbling
fuho illegal
fui suddenly
fujin lady
fu-jiyū inconvenient; needy; weak
fukai, f'kai deep
fukin, f'kin napkin, towel, cloth
fuku, f'ku blows; wipes clothes, suit, dress
fukuro, f'kuro bag, sack

fukushū, f'kushū review
fukuzatsu, f'kuzatsu complicated
fuman discontented, dissatisfied
fumei unknown, obscure
fumimas, fumu steps on
fun minute
funayoi seasick(ness)
fune boat
fun-iki atmosphere
Furansu France
furemas', fureru touches, comes in contact with
furi manner, air, pretense
furimas', furu waves, shakes, wags
furimasu rain, snow
furo bath
furōnin vagabond, tramp
furu second-hand
furui old
furyō bad, no good
fūryū elegant
fusagimas', fusagu stop up, closes, blocks
fusawasnii suitable, worthy; becoming
fusegimas', fusegu prevents; defends, protects
fushigi strange; wonderful; suspicious
fusoku shortage, deficiency, scarcity
futari, f'tari two persons
futatsu, f'tatsu two; two years old
futo, f'to unexpectedly
futoi, f'toi fat, plump
futsuka two days
fuyu winter

G

ga (subject particle) who does, what is
ga but; and
ga arimasu there is, are (for inanimate things)
ga imasu there is, there are (for living things)

gai damage, harm, injury
gaijin foreigner (usually American or European)
gaikō-kan diplomat
gaikoku abroad; foreign countries
Gaimu-shō Ministry of Foreign Affairs
gakkō school
gaku learning, study, science
gakumon knowledge, learning, education
gakusei, gak'sei student, schoolboy
gakusha, gak'sha scholar
gamaguchi pocketbook,
gaman shimas' is patient, puts up with
gaman dekimasen (dekinai) can't stand it
gan-yaku a pill
garasu glass
gasorin gasoline
gasu, gas' gas
gehin vulgar
gei arts, accomplishments; tricks; stunts
geijutsu art(s)
geisha a geisha girl
geki play, drama
gekijō theater
gekkyū monthly salary
gemmitsu strictly
gendai modern, up-to-date
gengo language
gen-in cause, origin, root
genki in good health, well
genki desu I'm fine
genkin, gen-nama cash, ready money
genshi (-bakudan) atom (bomb)
genzai the present (time)
genzo shimas' develops (film)
geppu monthly instalments
geri diarrhoea
geshuku lodgings; board and room
-getsu month
getsuyōbi Monday

gimon question, doubt
gimu duty, obligation
gin silver
ginkō bank
giri obligation, sense of obligation, honor
gishi engineer
-go language
gogatsu May
gogo p.m., afternoon
gohan cooked rice; meal; food
gohyaku five hundred
go-ju fifty
Gokigen yō Goodbye; Hello
goku very, exceedingly
goman fifty thousand
Gomen kudasai Hello—anybody home?
Gomen nasai Excuse me
gomi trash, rubbish, dust
gomu rubber
goran ... (you) look, see, try
goro about
gosen five thousand
Goshimpai naku! Don't worry about it.
go-yō your business
guai condition, shape, feelings (of health)
gumpuku military uniform
gun army, troops
gunjin soldier, military man
gunsō sergeant
gutai-teki concrete, substantial, tangible, material
gūzen accidentally
gyaku opposite, contrary
gyofu fisherman
gyōgi behaviour, manners
gyūniku beef
gyūnyū milk

H

ha tooth

haba width
habukimas' habuku cuts out,
  reduces, saves, eliminates, omits
hachi eight
hachi-gatsu August
hachi-jū eighty
hachinin eight people
hadaka naked
hadashi barefoot
hae housefly
hagaki postcard
hage bald
hageshii violent, severe
haha (my) mother
hai yes
hai-iro gray
haikara fashionable, high-class
  (slang)
hairimas', hairu enters; is inside
haitte imas' is inside
haitatsu delivery
haiyū actor
haizara ashtray
hajimarimas', hajimaru it begins
  (starts)
hajime the beginning; in the
  beginning
hajimete for the first time
Hajimemashite. How do you do?
hakari measuring scales
hakarimas', hakaru measures,
  weighs
hakimas' (haku) vomits; spits out,
  sweeps; wears on feet
hakkiri plainly, clearly, distinctly
hakkō publication
hako box
hakobimas' hakobu carries, conveys
hama beach
hamemas', hameru wears (on
  fingers)
han half, thirty minutes
hana flower
hana nose
hanaremas', hanareru separates,
  becomes

hanashi talk, story, tale
hanashimas' hanasu speaks, talks;
  lets loose, lets go, sets free
hane feather, wing
han-i scope, range
hantai opposite, contrary, reverse
happa leaf
hara belly, stomach
hara field
haraimas', harau pays; brushes
  aside, shakes out
haremas', hareru (weather) clears
  up, swells up
hari needle; hand (of clock)
haru springtime
hasami scissors, clippers
hashi bridge
hashi (o-hashi) chopsticks
hashigo ladder, stairs
hashirimas', hashiru runs
hassen eight thousand
hata flag
hatake field
hatakimas', hataku slap, beat; dust
hatarakimas', hataraku works
hatoba pier, wharf
hatsumei invention
hatsuon pronunciation
hattatsu development
hayai fast, quick, early
hayarimas', hayaru is popular, is in
  fashion
hayashi forest
hazu is expected to; is supposed to; is
  reasonable to expect
hazukashii ashamed
hebi snake
hedatarimas', hedataru is distant, is
  estranged
hei wall, fence
heiki calm, composed, cool,
  indifferent
heikin average
heitai soldier
heiwa peace
heizei usually, ordinarily, generally

hen (na) strange, odd, queer
hen vicinity, neighborhood
henji answer
henka change
herashimas', he-rasu decreases, cuts
  it down, shortens, curtails
heta unskilful, poor, inexpert
heya room
hi fire
hi day; sun
hidari left
hidoi severe, unreasonable, terrible
hidoku hard, cruelly, terribly
higashi east
hige beard, mustache
higeki tragedy
hiji elbow
hijō emergency
hijo ni extremely
hikaku comparison
hikidashi drawer
hiki-kaemasu, -kaeru exchanges,
  converts
hikōjō airport
hikoki airplane
hikō-yūbin airmail
hikui low, short
hima time; leisure, spare time
himitsu secret, mystery
hin quality; elegance, refinement,
  dignity
hirattai flat
Hirippin Philippines
hiroi wide, broad
hiroimas', hirou picks up
hiru daytime; noon
hiru kara from afternoon
hitai forehead, brow
hito person, man
hito- one
hitori one person
hitori de alone
hitoshii equal, identical, similar
hitsuyō necessity, need; necessary
hiya (o-hiya) cold water

hiyō cost, expense
hiyori weather; conditions
hiza knee, lap
hizuke date
hō law; rule; method
hōbi (go-hōbi) prize, reward
hōbō everywhere, all over,
  which way
hodo extent; limits; moderation;
  approximate time
hoka other, in addition to, other than
hoken insurance
hokori pride, boast
hokori dust
hoku- north
hōkyū pay, salary
hōmen direction, quarter, district
homemas', homeru praises
hommono the real thing
hōmon call, visit
hon book
hon- main; chief; this; the; present
hondō the main route
hone bone
honki serious, earnest
Honkon Hong Kong
honno a slight, just a little, a mere
honrai originally, from the start
hontō, honto true; truth; really
honyaku translation
hoppeta cheek
hoppō northern
horemas', horeru falls in love, takes
  a fancy
horidashi-mono a bargain, a real find
hōritsu law
horimas', horu digs, excavates
hoshi star
hoshii is desired; desires, wants
hoshō guarantee
hōsō (-kyoku) broadcast (station)
hosoi slender
hōtai bandage
hoteru hotel
hotondo almost (all); almost all the
  time

JAPANESE-ENGLISH

hyaku hundred
hyaku-man million
hyō table, schedule
hyōban reputation, fame
hyōgen expression (words)
hyōjō expression (on face)
hyōjun standard
hyōmen surface
hyotto accidentally, by chance
hyotto sh'tara maybe, possibly

I

i- medicine, doctoring
ian consolation; recreation
ichi one
ichi-ba market, marketplace
ichiban number one; first; best; most
ichibu a part, portion
ichido one time
ichi-gatsu January
ichi-ji one o'clock
ichijitsu one day; some day
ichiman ten thousand
ichinichi-ju all day
ido a well
ie a house
igai unexpected
igaku medicine, medical studies
Igirisu England
... igo afterwards, from ... on
ii good, fine
iie no
iimas, yū says
iimashita said
iin committee (member)
iin-kai committee
ii-wake explanation, excuse
iji temper, disposition
ijō unusual
... ika below, less than ...
ikaga how (about it)?
ikaga desu ka how do you like?
ikagawashii suspicious, questionable, shady

ikari anger
ike pond
ikebana flower arrangement
ikemasen, ikenai it won't do; you musn't; don't
iken opinion
iki breath
iki (na) smart, stylish
ikioi vigor, energy, spirit
ikimas', iku goes
ikiru (ikite imas') lives, is alive
ik-ko one (piece)
ikura how much
ikutsu how many; how old
ima now
imas', iru is, stays
imi meaning
imōto (my) younger sister
in seal, stamp
inai within
inaka country
inchiki fake, fraud
Indo India
Indoneshiya Indonesia
infure inflation
inki ink
inki (na) gloomy
inochi one's life
inori prayer
inshō impression
interi intellectual; highbrow
inu dog
ippai full; a cupful (glassful)
... irai since ...
Irasshai(mase)! Welcome!
irasshaimas', irassharu (someone honored) comes; goes; stays, is
ireba false teeth
iremas', ireru puts in, lets in
iriguchi entrance
irimas', iru is necessary; needs; wants
iro color; sex
isha doctor, physician
ishi will, intention

63

ishi stone
isogashii busy
isogimas', isogu hurries, rushes
issai all, everything, without exception
issaku-ban(-jitsu) night (day) before last
issho (ni) together with
isshō one's whole life
isshō-kemmei desperately; very hard
isshu a kind, a sort
isu chair
ita board, plank
itai painful, hurting
itami an ache, a pain
itashimas', itasu I (humbly) do
itazura mischief, prank
itchi agreement
ito thread, yarn; silk
itoko cousin
itsu when
itsu-ka 5 days; 5th day; sometime
itsu made until when
itsutsu five
itsuwari falsehood, lie
ittai ... on earth, ... indeed
ittei fixed, settled, definite
ittō first, first class
iwai celebration, party
iwayuru so-called, what you might call
iya no
iya (na) unpleasant; disagreeable; disliked
iyashii lowly, vulgar
iyo-iyo at last; in fact; more and more
izen since, before, ago

J

ja, jā well, well then; in that case; now
ja arimasen (ja nai) it is not; it is not a case of
jama interference, disturbance, hindrance, obstacle

ji a letter; a Chinese character
ji land, ground; texture; fabric
ji haemorrhoids
-ji o'clock
jibiki dictionary
jibun oneself; myself; alone
jidai age, period, era, time
jidō-teki automatic
jihen incident, happening
jijō circumstances; conditions
jikan time; hour
jika ni directly; personally
jiki ni immediately; soon
jikken experiment
jikkō performance; practice; realization
jiko accident
jiman pride, boast
jimi plain, sober
jimū business, office work
jimuin office clerk
jimusho office
-jin person
jinkō population
jisatsu suicide
jishin earthquake
jishin self-confidence
jissai actual conditions, reality; in practice; in fact, really
jitensha bicycle
jitsu truth; truly, really
jitsugyō business, industry
jitsugyo-ka businessman
jiyū freedom, free; fluent, at ease
jōbu healthy, sturdy
jochū maid-servant
jōdan joke
jokyū waitress
jōriku disembarking, landing
jōsha getting into a car, boarding
... joshi Madame, Miss, Mrs.
jōshiki common sense
jōtai condition, situation, circumstances
jōtō the best, first-rate
jōzu skilled, clever, good at

JAPANESE-ENGLISH

ju ten
ju gun
jūbun enough
jū-hachi eighteen
jū-ichi eleven
jūku nineteen
jū-man a hundred thousand
jumbi preparations
jun order, turn
jun (na) pure
jū-ni twelve
junsa policeman
jū-roku sixteen
jusan thirteen
jushi/juyon fourteen
jushichi/junana seventeen
jūsu orange soda pop; juice
jūtan rug, carpet
jūyo importance
juzu beads

K

ka question particle
kabe wall
kabu stock (in a company)
kachimas', katsu wins
kaemas', kaeru changes, exchanges
kaerimas', kaesu goes home, goes
   back
kaeshimas', kaesu returns it
kagaku science
kagami mirror
kagi key
kagimas', kagu smells it
kagiri limit, extent
kago basket
kagu furniture
kai a meeting
kaidan steps, stairs
kaigai overseas, abroad
kaikan a public hall, a building
kaikei accounts
kaimas', kau buys
kaimono shopping

kaisha company
kaiwa conversation
kaji a fire
kakemas', kakeru multiplies
kakimas', kaku writes; scratches
kakitome registered mail
kami hair (on the head)
kami paper
kanai my wife
kanarazu for sure
kanari fairly, rather
kanashii sad
kane money; metal; bell
kangae thought; idea; opinion
kangaemas', kangaeru thinks
kangofu nurse
kanji feeling
kanjō bill
kankō sightseeing
kankōkyaku tourist
kanōsei possibility
kansha thanks, gratitude
kanshin concern, interest
kanshin shimas' admires
kantan simple
kanzei customs duty
kao face; looks, a look
kara empty
... kara from; since; because, so
karada body
kare he, him
kare-ra they, them
kari temporary
kasa umbrella
kasegimas', kasegu earns, works for
   (money)
kasu (kashimas') lends
kata person, honored person
katachi form, shape
katai hard; strong; upright; strict
katana sword
katarimas', kataru relates, tells
katei home, household, family
katte kitchen
kawa skin

kawari change, substitute
kawase a money order
kayōbi Tuesday
kaze wind; a cold
kazoemas', kazoeru counts
kazu number
kega wound, injury
keiei management, operation
keiken experience
keiko exercise, practice, drill
keisatsu police
keiyaku contract, agreement
kekka result; as a result
  (consequence)
kekkon marriage
kembutsu sightseeing
kenka quarrel
kenkō health
keredo(mo) however, though, but
kesseki absent
kesshin determination, resolution
kesu (keshimas') puts out; turns off;
  erases
kibō hope
ki-chigai mad, insane
ki-iro yellow
kikai chance, opportunity
kiken danger, peril
kikō climate
kimi you
kimyō strange, peculiar
kin gold
kinjo neighbourhood, vicinity
kinō yesterday
kinshi prohibition, ban
kin-yōbi Friday
kippu ticket
kiroku record
kiryo personal appearance, looks;
  ability
kisetsu season
kisha newspaperman, reporter
kishi shore, coast, bank
kita north
kitanai dirty

kizashi symptoms, signs, indications
ko child; person
kōba factory
kobamimas', kobamu refuses,
  rejects; opposes, resists
kochira here; this way; this one; me,
  I; us, we
kōdō action, hehaviour
kōfuku happiness
kōfun excitement
kōgeki attack
kōgi lecture
koi love
koibito sweetheart
koitsu this one
kokku cook
koko here, this place
kokonotsu nine
kokonoka 9 days; the 9th day
kōkoku advertisement
kokoro mind, heart, spirit, feeling
kokumin a people, a nation
kokusai international
kokuseki nationality
Komban wa. Good evening
kome rice
komori bat
kon dark blue
kondo this time; next time
kongetsu this month
konnan difficulty, trouble, hardship
Konnichi wa. Good afternoon.
  (Hello)
kono this
kōri ice
kōri baggage
koshi-kakemas', kakeru sits down
kōsui perfume
kotoshi this year
kōtsū communication; traffic
koyama hill
kozutsumi package, parcel
ku nine
kubi neck
kudamono fruit

kudari down, going down; descent
... kudasai please
kugatsu September
kuimas, kuu eats
kūki air
kuma bear
kumiawase assortment, mixture
kumo cloud
kuni country; native place, home area
kurabemas', kuraberu compares,
    contrasts
kurabu club
kurai dark, gloomy
kurasu class
Kurisumasu Christmas
kuroi black
kurōto expert, professional
kuruma car; taxi; vehicle
kusuri, k'suri medicine
kutsu shoes
kutsu-shita socks
kyabarē cabaret, nightclub
kyaku (o-kyaku) visitor, guest,
    customer
kyō today
kyōdai brothers and sisters; brother;
    sister
kyōiku education
kyoku office, bureau
kyonen last year
kyori distance
kyōshi teacher, instructor, tutor
kyūji waiter, waitress, steward,
    office-boy
kyūyo compensation, allowance,
    grant

M

ma room; space; time; leisure
mā well; I should say; perhaps, good
    gracious
machi town
machigai mistake
machimas', matsu waits for

mado window
mae front; in front of; before
mago grandchild, grandson
mai- each
maiasa every morning
maiban every night
maido every time
mainen every year
mainichi every day; all the time
majime serious, sober
makoto sincere; faithful; true;
    genuine
makura pillow
mamorimas', mamoru defends,
    protects
man ten thousand
manekimas', maneku invites
mari ball
maru circle, ring; zero
marui round
massugu straight
mata again; moreover
mato aim, target
matomemas', matomeru settles,
    arranges
matsuri a festival
me eye; bud
mei niece
mekata weight
mekura blind
menkai interview, meeting
michi street, road
midori green
migi right
migoto splendid, beautiful
mikka 3 days; 3rd day
mikomi promise, hope; expectation;
    opinion
mimas', miru sees, looks; tries doing
mimi ear
minami south
minzoku race
miruku milk
mise store, shop
misemas', miseru shows

67

mittsu three
miyage a present, a souvenir
miyako capital, city
mochiron of course
moji letter, character, writing
mokuteki aim, objective, purpose
mokuyōbi Thursday
mokuyoku bathing
mondai question, problem, topic
moshi if
moshi moshi! hello! hey! say
motte ikimas' (iku) takes
muika 6 days; the 6th day
muko son-in-law; bridegroom
mura village
muryō free of charge
musuko, mus'ko son
musume daughter; girl
muttsu six
myōgonichi day after tomorrow
myōnichi tomorrow

N

nagai, nagaku long
nagemas', nageru throws
naifu knife
nakama friend, pal
namae name
namakemas', namakeru idles, is
    lazy
nami ordinary, common, average
nana(tsu) seven
nan(i) what
nan-, nam- how many ...
nanibun anyway, anyhow
nanoka 7 days; the 7th day
naraimas', narau learns
natsu summer
naze why
neko cat
nemurimas', nemuru sleeps
nen year
ni two
nibui dull

Nichi- Japanese
nichiyōbi Sunday
Nihon Japan
Nihon-jin a Japanese
Nihongo Japanese (language)
nii-san big brother
niji rainbow
ni-jū twenty; double, duplicate
nikoniko smiling
niku meat
ningen human being
nise phony, imitation
niwa garden
niwatori chicken
nodo throat
nomimas', nomu drinks
noroi slow, dull
nozomashii desirable, welcome
nyūsu news
nyūyoku hot bath, taking a hot bath

O

ō- big, great
oba(san) aunt; lady
obāsan grandmother; old lady
ochimas' ochiru falls; drops; is
    omitted; falls; runs away; is
    inferior
odorimas', odoru dances
oemas', oeru finishes, completes
Ohayō (gozaimas') Good morning
o-hiya cold water
oi nephew
oishii tasty, nice, delicious
oji (san) uncle
ojii-san grandfather
okami landlady, woman
o-kane money
okāsan mother
okimas' okiru gets up
okonaimas', okonau acts, does,
    carries out, performs
ōku lots; mostly
okurimono gift, present

JAPANESE-ENGLISH

omedetō (gozaimas')
    congratulations; happy new year
omocha toy
omoi heavy; important
omou thinks; feels
on obligation; kindness
on sound; pronunciation
onaji same
onaka stomach
onaka ga s'kimash'ta is hungry
ondo temperature
ongaku music
onore self
orimono textiles, cloth
oshiire closet, cupboard
Ōshū Europe
osoi late; slow
osoreirimas'-excuse me; thank you
osu (oshimas') pushes
oto sound, noise
otoko man, male, boy
otona adult
otōtō younger brother
ototoi day before yesterday
ototoshi year before last
oya parent

P

pan bread
pēji page
penki paint
pinto focus
poketto pocket
pūru swimming pool; motor pool,
    parking lot

R

raigetsu next month
raikyaku guest, caller, visitor
rainen next year
raishu next week
raku ease, comfort, comfortable
rakudai failure (in a test)
rei (o-rei) greeting; thanks

reigi courtesy
reizōko refrigerator, icebox
rekishi history
rekōdo record
ren-ai love
renshū training, practice, drill
ressha a train
ri advantage, profit, interest
rikai understanding, comprehension
rikō clever, sharp
riku land
rikutsu reason, logic, argument
ringo apple
rishi interest
riyū reason
roku six
rōsoku candle
ryōhō both
ryoken passport
ryōkō travel, trip
ryokyaku traveler, passenger
ryōshin both parents

S

sā well; come on
sabishii lonely
... sae even; only
saifu purse
saigo last, final
saijō best, highest
saiwai good fortune
saji spoon
sakemas', sakeru avoids
sampo a walk
san three
-san Mr., Mrs., Miss
sansei approval, support
saru monkey
satō sugar
sayonara goodbye
seifu government
seikatsu life
seikō success
seisan production, manufacture

seito pupil, student
sekai world
seki cough
sekinin responsibility, obligation
sekken soap
semai narrow
sen thousand
sengetsu last month
sensei teacher
senshū last week
setsumei explanation
setsuna moment, instant
sewashii busy
sha-in employee
shan pretty, handsome
shashin photo, picture
shi death
shichi seven
shichi-jū seventy
shigatsu April
shi-jū forty
shimas', suru does
shimasen doesn't
shimin citizen
shimpai worry, uneasiness
shimpo progress
shindai bed, berth
shinnen new year
shinrai trust, confidence
shinrui relative
shinsetsu kind, cordial
shinzō heart
shirase report, notice
shirmas', shiru knows
shiroi white
shishi lion
shita, sh'ta bottom, below, under
shita, sh'ta tongue
shita, sh'ta did, has gone
shitaku, sh'taku preparation,
  arrangement
shitsumon question
shizuka quiet, still
shōbai trade, business
shōhin goods, merchandise

shōjiki honest
shoki secretary
shōko proof, evidence
shokumotsu food
shomei signature
shōni infant, child
shōrai future
shoseki books, publications
shōtai invitation
shotchū all the time
shoten bookshop
shōyo bonus, prize, reward
shozai whereabouts
shū(-kan) week
shudan ways, means, measures, steps
shujin boss, master; husband
shūkan custom, practice, habit
shukuga congratulation
shūmatsu weekend
shuppatsu departure
shūri repair
shurui kind, sort
shūshoku getting a job
shusseki attendance, presence
shutchō a business trip, an official
  tour
sō that's right, yes; that way, like that
Sō des' ka Oh? How interesting
Is that right?
sōbetsu farewell; send-off
sochira there, that way; that one
sofu grandfather
sōji cleaning, sweeping
sokkuri entirely, completely; just like
son damage, loss, disadvantage
sono that
sora sky
sore that one, it
sōron quarrel, dispute
soshiki system, structure
soto outside, outdoors
sōzō imagination
sū number; numeral
subarashii wonderful
subete all

JAPANESE-ENGLISH

suiei swimming
suifu seaman, sailor
suiyōbi Wednesday
sukkari completely, all
sukuimas', sukuu helps, rescues,
saves
sumashimas', sumasu finishes,
concludes; puts up with (things) as
they are)
Sumimasen Excuse me; Thank you.
sumpō measurements
suna sand
sune shin, leg
supōtsu, s'pōts sports, athletics
suru (shimas') does
susumemas', susumeru encourages,
recommends, advises, persuades,
urges
suteki, s'teki fine, splendid, swell
sutemas', suteru throws away,
abandons
suzushii cool

T

tabemas', taberu eats
tabemono food
tabi journey, trip
tabi-tabi often
tabun probably, likely, perhaps; a lot
tada only, just; (for) free, ordinary
tadaima just now; in a minute
tadashii proper, correct, honest
-tai wants to, is eager to
taiken personal experience
taira even, smooth, flat
taisetsu important, precious
taishi ambassador
taishi-kan embassy
taishū the general public, the masses;
pópular
takai high; loud, expensive
takara a treasure
takumi skill
tama ni rarely, occasionally, seldom

tamago egg
tame for the sake (good, benefit) of;
for the purpose of; because (of)
tamemas', tameru accumulates
tameshimas', tamesu tries, attempts,
experiments with
tana shelf, rack
tango words, vocabulary
tanjōbi birthday
tanoshii pleasant, enjoyable
taoru towel
tarai tub, basin
tarimas, tariru is enough, suffices
taryō large quantity
tassha healthy; skillful, good at
tasshimas', tassuru accomplishes;
reaches
tasū large number; majority
tatakaimas', tatakau fights
tatemono building
tatoeba for example, for instance
tayori communication,
correspondence, a letter, word from
tazunemas', tazuneru asks (a
question); visits; looks for
te hand, arm; trick, move; kind
tēburu table
tēburu no ue on top of the table, on
the table
tegami letter
te-gatai safe; reliable; steady
tehazu arrangements
teinei polite; careful
te-ire repair; upkeep
teishu host; landlord; husband
tejun order, procedure, program
tekazu trouble
teki enemy, opponent, rival
tekigi suitable, fit
tekitō suitable
te-kubi wrist
temae this side
... -te mo even if ..., however
tenpi oven
-ten shop

tenki weather; nice weather
te-nugui hand towel
teppen top
teppō rifle
tēpu tape
tēpurekoda tape recorder
terebi television
terimas', teru it shines
tesage handbag
tetsu iron, steel
tetsudaimas', tetsudau helps
to door
tōchaku arrival
tochi ground; a piece of land
todokimas', todoku reaches, arrives
todomarimas', todomaru stops;
  remains
togamemas', togameru blames,
  reproves, finds fault with
togemas', togeru achieves,
  accomplishes
tōi far-off, distant
toimas', tou inquires
toire(tto) toilet
tōka 10 days; 10th day
tokai city, town
tokei clock; watch
toki time
toko bed
tokoro place; address; circumstance,
  time
tomo together; company; friend
tonari next-door, neighbouring
tora tiger
tori chicken; bird
torimas', toru takes; takes away
tōroku registration
toshi age; year
toshi-shita younger
toshi-ue older
toshiyori an aged person
to(t) temo terribly, extremely,
  completely
totsuzen suddenly
totte kimas' (kuru) brings

totte ikimas' (iku) takes
tsū authority, expert
tsuchi report, notice
tsugemas', tsugeru tells, informs
tsūjō usually, generally
tsuki, ts'ki moon
tsuma wife
tsumetai cold (to the touch)
tsura face
tsure company, companion
tsūshin correspondence; news
tsūyaku interpreter; interpreting
tsuyoi strong; brave
tsuzuku to continue
tsuzukimas' continues

U

uchi house, home; family inside;
  among
uchiki shy, timid
ude arm
ude-kubi wrist
ude-wa bracelet
ue above, upper; on top of
ugokimas', ugoku moves
uji family, clan; family name
ukagaimas', ukagau visits; asks a
  question; hears; looks for
ukemas', ukeru receives; accepts;
  takes; gets; suffers
uke-tsuke information desk;
  receptionist
umaremas', umareru is born
umpan transportation
un fate, luck
undō movement; exercise; sports;
  athletics
uo fish
uremas', ureru sells, is in demand;
  thrives; is popular
ureshii delightful, pleasant,
  wonderful
urimas', uru sells
uru wool

JAPANESE-ENGLISH

urusai annoying
ushi cow, cattle
ushiro behind; (in) back
usui thin, pale, weak
uta song; poem
utagaimas', utagau doubts
utsukushii beautiful
uwabaki slippers
uwa-gaki address
uwagi coat, jacket
uwasa rumor, gossip

W

wabi apology
wabishii miserable; lonely
wadai topic of conversation
waga-mama selfish
waishatsu shirt
wakai young
wakarimas', wakaru it is clear
  (understood); understands; has
  good sense
wake reason; meaning; case,
  circumstance
wampaku naughty
waraimas', warau laughs
ware onself; me
ware-ware we; us
waribiki discount
warui bad; at fault
wa-shoku Japanese food
wasuremono leaving something
  behind; a thing left behind
wasuremas', wasureru forgets
watakushi, watashi I, me
watashi-tachi we, us

Y

... ya and; or
yā hi!, hello!
yabai dangerous (will get you into
  trouble)
yachin house rent

yagate before long; in time
yahari also; either; all the same
yake desperation
yakkai trouble, bother
yakkyoku pharmacy
yakuhin drugs; chemicals
yakume duty, function
yakusho government office
yamashii ashamed or guilty-feeling
Yamato Japan
yamimas', yamu it stops
yamome widow
yamu-o-enai unavoidable
yappari also; either; all the same
... yara ... or something; what with ...
yarimas', yaru gives; sends, does
yasai vegetables
yasashii gentle; easy
yasumi rest, break; vacation; holiday
yatoimas', yatou employs, hires
yattsu eight
yaya a little; a little while
yo- four
yobimas', yobu calls; names;
  summons; invites
yoi the (early) evening
yōjin precaution, caution, care
yōka 8 days; 8th day
yokemas', yokeru avoids, keeps
  away from
yōki cheerful, bright, lively
yokin deposit (of money), bank
  account
yokka 4 days; 4th day
yoku well; lots, much
yoku- the next day
yome bride
yomimas', yomu reads
yon four
yo-nin 4 people
... yori that; from; since
yoroshii very well; excellent
yoroshiku, yorosh'ku one's regards,
  one's best wishes
yoru night

73

Yosh'! OK!
yoshi reason; meaning; circumstances; means
yoshimas', yosu stop it
yōsu circumstances; aspect; appearance, look
yō-tashi business, errand
yotei expectation, plan
yottsu four
yoyaku reservation, subscription, booking
yōyaku gradually; at last; barely
yūbe last night
yubi finger; toe
yūbi elegant, graceful
yūbi-kyoku post office
yubiwa ring
yue reason, grounds
yuki snow
yukkuri slowly; at ease
yūkō effective, valid
yūme dream
yumei famous
yūri profitable, advantageous
yūryoku strong, powerful, influential
yūshō victory, championship
yūshoku supper
yushutsu export(ing)
yusō transport(ation)
yuzu orange, citron

Z

zadan chat
zaisan property
zaisei finance
zannen regret, disappointed; too bad
zara-ni found everywhere, very common
zara-zara rough
zaseki seat
zashiki room, living room
zasshi magazine, periodical
zatto roughly; briefly
zehi without fail, for sure; right or wrong
zeikin tax
zembu all
zempō the front
zen- all, total, complete, the whole
zento the future, prospects
zen-ya the night before
zenzen completely, utterly, entirely, altogether
zetsubō despair
zōka increase, growth
zu picture, drawing, map, diagram
zubon trousers, pants
zunō brains, head
zuru cheating
zutsū headache
zutto directly; by far, much (more); all through, all the time
zusan sloppy, slipshod, careless

TRAVEL GUIDE TO JAPAN

FOCUS ON TOKYO

Recorded by
**Christopher Side B.A. (Hons) &
Penny Ann Strange TEFL**

TOWARDS A BETTER HOLIDAY

Shoppers in Ginza, Tokyo.

Millions have begun to leave home to explore the world they came to know through television, radio and books. Airports can no longer hold them and airlines are bidding for bigger and faster aircraft. New opportunities abound for businessmen and travellers to explore the world.

At Europhone Institute our aim has been to constantly upgrade our publications and educational products to give better value to our patrons. Following the addition of dictionaries to all our language teaching books, the creation of this section on travel information is our latest innovation.

We hope this section will equip travellers to avoid the pitfalls peculiar to each country. Hopefully they will be sensitive to the way of life in the host country and harmonise with the people and their culture. A better holiday and more favourable responses from the people they meet will be their reward — a step towards better international understanding and goodwill. *Have a Good Holiday!*

Publishers

CONTENTS

1

PLANNING THE TRIP

An Airport Limousine (bus).

Avoiding the Crowds

For a pleasant travel in Japan, it is best to avoid the undermentioned peak seasons for travel. First there is a mass exodus of people from the cities to the countryside and then a return from their holidays. Ferries, trains, airlines and lodgings will be filled to capacity. If you must travel during these periods, make your bookings six months in advance.

a   New Year Holiday Season
    27 December to 4 January and adjacent weekends
b   Golden Week Holiday Season
    29 April to 5 May and adjacent weekends
c   Bon Festival
    a week centering around 15 August

Immigration

Holders of a valid passport may apply to the nearest Japanese Embassy or Consulate for a tourist visa. The period of stay normally granted is 90 days. Two copies of the application

A taxi in Tokyo.

must be submitted, each with a recent passport size photograph and a return air or sea ticket to Japan. Nationals of countries with reciprocal visa exemptions need not obtain a visa for a stay of between two weeks to six months.

Customs Formalities

An oral declaration that one has no dutiable goods is normally sufficient. However, a written declaration is necessary if the visitor comes by ship, has unaccompanied baggage or brings dutiable goods in excess of the duty-free allowance. Duty payment is waived on personal effects and professional equipment so long as the quantities are reasonable. The following duty-free goods may be imported by each foreigner: 400 cigarettes, 500 grams of tobacco or 100 cigars; three bottles of alcoholic beverages (760 cc each), two ounces of perfume and gifts not exceeding 200,000 Yen.

Health Regulations

No innoculations are necessary for tourists visiting Japan.

2

MAKING THE MOST OF YOUR STAY

Currency

The local currency is the Yen (¥). US$1 was equivalent to 145 Yen on 1st April, 1990. Coins have values of ¥1,000, ¥500, ¥100, ¥50, ¥10, ¥5 and ¥1. Notes come in ¥10,000, ¥5,000 and ¥1,000 denominations. Japanese currency may be purchased at banks, major hotels and airports. Visitors may import any amount of foreign and Japanese currency. They may export an unlimited amount of foreign currency but only five million Yen.

Airport Tax

A payment of 2000 Yen is necessary as airport tax for departing visitors.

Heading for the City

The majority of tourists use the efficient Airport Limousine bus service to get to Tokyo. It is cheaper than using a taxi. The service from Narita Airport to the city which takes less than two hours costs 2500 Yen. Tickets are sold at the Limousine Counter at airports.

Tipping

Tipping is not customary. Hotel porters, waiters, taxi drivers and other service personnel do not expect tips.

Taxis

Taxis are the most convenient means of travel. They may be stopped at undesignated places. In Tokyo the fare is ¥480 for the first two kilometres and ¥80 for every 370 metres thereafter. After 11 pm and until 5 am, a surcharge of 20% is payable.

Mailing

Post offices operate from 9 am to 5 pm, Monday to Friday. On Saturdays, only the larger post offices open from 9 am to 12.30 pm for mailing services but not for financial transactions. Mailing services are available at most hotels and letters with stamps may be dropped in any public mail box.

Public Telephones

Public telephones are coloured green, red, pink, blue and yellow. Yellow, green and red phones with gold bands are more suitable for long distance calls as the coin box accepts ¥100 coins. Local calls cost ¥10 and it is advisable to insert several coins to avoid being interrupted after three minutes. Phone cards may be purchased for ¥500, ¥1,000, ¥3,000 or ¥5,000 at the offices of the Nippon Telegraph & Telephone Corporation, at department stores and from vending machines.

International Calls

International calls may be made from hotels and public phones through the operator or by making direct ISD (International Subscriber Dialling) calls. ISD calls are cheaper than operator assisted calls. ISD calls may be made from green public telephones with an "International Domestic Card/Coin Telephone" legend on the coin box. To activate the service the caller has to pick up the receiver and insert ¥100 coins or a telephone card. Then he has to dial: 001 + Country Code + Area Code + Local Telephone No.

Banks

Banks open from 9 am to 3 pm, Monday to Friday and close on Saturdays, Sundays and Public Holidays. Tourists must produce their passports when they wish to cash travellers' cheques or purchase Japanese currency from a "Foreign Exchange Authorised Bank."

Air, Rail & Subways

Japan is serviced by three domestic airlines which cover the entire country. They are Japan Airlines, All Nippon Airways and Japan Air Systems. Japan Railways and regional lines are alternatives to air and long-distance bus travel. The Tokyo subway is a fast and efficient service. Maps in English are displayed at all stations. Tourists who are unable to determine the correct fare need only purchase the cheapest ticket. The difference can be paid at the destination.

3

WHAT TO SEE

A city scene in Tokyo.

Tokyo is the largest city in the world being 2,145 sq. kilometres in area (1,341 sq. miles), about twice the size of Greater London. Its population is quoted as 12 million but some sources believe this to be only an approximate figure of Japan's 120 million. Forty-three places of interest have been identified. All of them may be reached by the Airport Limousine or subway. Free copies of the Limousine City Guide are available at the Limousine Counter at airports. The Guide contains a map of the city of Tokyo with its subway lines, bus stops and 43 places of interest. Eleven of these places are described below.

Tokyo Tower

Tourists can enjoy a stunning view of the city from two platforms on the Tokyo Tower; the first is at a height of 150 metres and the second at 250 metres. The tower doubles as a multiple radio and television transmitting centre. At the base there is a TV station, a science museum and an aquarium.

Japanese opera in progress.

Old Japan

To savour the atmosphere of old Japan, visitors will enjoy the picturesque downtown district of *Asakusa* with the oldest temple in Tokyo, the Sensoji Temple. A gigantic gate at its entrance with an even more imposing paper lantern welcomes tourists to a passway that leads to the temple amidst interesting souvenir shops.

Buddhist Shrine

The shogan of Tokugawa displayed his great wealth and power by building an imposing family temple in the Shiba Koen district of Tokyo. Occupying 85,000 sq metres, it is today the Zojoji Temple of the Jodo Buddhists of Japan.

Wholesale Fish Market

Early risers and night-owls may wish to visit the huge fish market in Tsukiji. The biggest in Japan, it is interesting to watch the bidders pitting their wits against the auctioneers.

3

Ueno Park and Zoo

The park attains its full glory at cherry blossom time when it is visited by hordes of children and adults. The park includes the Shinobazu Pond, Ueno Zoo and the National Museum of Western Art and Natural History.

NHK Broadcasting Centre

For a free conducted tour of the television studios of the NHK (Japan Broadcasting Corporation), visit it any day of the week to witness actual filming in its East and West buildings. The centre houses five radio and television stations.

National Museum of Western Art

Art lovers can feast their eyes on an extensive collection of French impressionist paintings and over 50 sculptures of Rodin at this museum. Not far away is the Tokyo Culture Hall (Tokyo Bunka Kaikan), the National Science Museum, and the Enono Mori Art Museum. To visit these places, a strategic disembarkation point for the subway traveller is the Keisei Ueno Station or the Tokyo Metropolitan Station.

Zoo with Pandas

The Ueno Zoo has over 300 specimens of animals. It is the biggest in Japan and draws an unending stream of animal lovers and tourists. The star attraction is the panda. The zoo is served by a monorail which connects it to an adjacent aquarium. The aquatic zoo called "the pond" (shinoba zunoike) is in another location and may be reached by disembarking at the Yushima Station along the Chiyoda Line.

Financial Centre

Marunouchi is Tokyo's financial district. It is a prestigious location for local and overseas companies. The head offices of Japan's major trading houses and banks are located there. Marunouchi grew in importance after the opening of the Tokyo Centre Station. *Nihonbashi* is another business district with many stores of repute which have been in existence since the Edo Period.

Edo Castle

This shogan's castle was built in 1457 during the Edo Period of military dictatorship. In 1888 it became the Imperial Palace and was damaged during the second world war. Rebuilt in 1968, it is now the residence of the emperor and his consort. Entry into the palace is restricted to two visits a year – on New Year's Day and on the Emperor's Birthday (29th April). On these occasions the royal family will make appearances at their balcony to wave to the crowds below.

Disneyland, Tokyo

Disneyland which is at Urayasu is a prime attraction in Tokyo. There is a direct Limousine bus service to it from Narita Airport. The park's attractions are similar to those in the parent park in California. Visitors are forewarned of the long queues for the purchase of admission tickets. Conditions are at their worst during weekends, school and public holidays and in summer.

SOME NATIONAL ATTRACTIONS

The Kegon Water Fall

The Kegon Falls is the most famous of Japan's three waterfalls. It is a spectacle to watch the gusty winds turn the roaring waters into lace-like drapery. Tourists wanting an unusual experience may take the lift to the bottom of the gorge to gaze at the 99 metre drop of the waterfall.

Lake Chuzenji

In the shadow of Mt Nantai lies Lake Chuzenji which is 11.5 sq km in area and 21 km in circumference. The lake came into being 1270 metres above sea level following the eruption of Mt Nantai. The lake is a popular fishing ground that is plentifully supplied with salmon and rainbow trout. Nature lovers visit it for its scenery.

Volcanic Mountains

For the adventurous the Hakone mountain tour is recommended. A view of Mt Fuji will be possible during the journey. The reflection of Mt Fuji on Lake Ashi (Ashinoko)

3

A view of Mount Fuji.

is a sight not to be missed. A ride on a sight-seeing boat will ensure a good view. The best view is from the Owakudani observatory which is 1050 metres above sea level. Not far away is the site of the eruption of the Hakone volcano. Visitors will smell sulphur in the air and see spurts of steam rise above the ground. Komagatake (1327 metres) is the core of the Hakone volcanic mountains and is linked by a cable car that takes visitors to a skate centre and an old shrine.

Travelling In and Out of Japan

A list of international and domestic airlines with their telephone numbers is printed in the page marked *List of Airlines*.

Handling Emergencies

In the event of sickness or other mishaps, readers may refer to the page entitled, *If You Need Help*. A list of hospitals and other useful telephone numbers are included. A list of embassies appears in the *List of Embassies in Tokyo*.

WHERE TO STAY IN TOKYO

The Ginza Dai-ichi Hotel.

In the cities, Western-type hotels exist. Although the rooms are small, efficient service can be expected. A 10 percent service charge is levied and tipping is not necessary.

Luxury hotels include the following:

1 Imperial Hotel, Tokyo   Tel (03) 504-1111
2 Grand Palace, Kudan Tokyo Tel (03) 264-1111
3 Le Pacific Meridian Tokyo Tel (03) 445-6711
4 Mikado Hotel, Tokyo   Tel (03) 447-3111
5 Century Hyatt, Tokyo   Tel (03) 349-0111

Moderately priced hotels which provide good value for money include:

1 Ginza Dai-ichi Hotel   Tel 03 (5425311), Fax 5010907
  8-13-A Ginza, 104, Tokyo
  Single Rooms from US$100   or   ¥15,000 + 16%
  Double Rooms from US$120   or   ¥18,000 + 16%

4

2   Grand Central Hotel, Tokyo   Tel (03) 256-3211
    Single Rooms from US$53   ¥8,000 + 16%
    Double Rooms from US$100   ¥15,000 + 16%
    There are 200 rooms and it is 5 minutes from the Ginza.

Business Hotels are a no-frills alternative for budget conscious travellers. Room service is not available and often even a coffee shop is not on the premises. However, most of these hotels are close to major railway stations or town centres with lots of restaurants in the vicinity. The rooms are very small with a bed. However it would always have a cubicle with a shower, bath and Western-style lavatory. For information on the location of such lodgings, call Japan Airport Terminal Co Ltd, Heneda Airport Departure Lobby on (03) 7478040, Fax (03) 747-1688.

A *ryokan* is a Japanese inn. The floor of the room is covered by a Tatami-mat and meals are served by a maid. Bedding will be provided (futon) for sleeping. Ryokans provide breakfast and dinner and the menu is determined by the management. Single guests are allotted a room each. However couples arriving together will be normally given one room regardless of their relationship. Dinner is served at 6–7 o'clock, early enough for the guests to get a snack outside if they find the food not to their liking. For more information, look for the counter of the Japan Airport Terminal Co Ltd at the airport. For Haneda Airport the Tel No is (03) 7478040, Fax No (03) 747-1688.

A *minshuku* is a lodging house with fewer facilities. The guest is expected to lay out his bedding. Such accomodation is found in the rural parts of the country and costs less than a *ryokan*. Government lodging houses are called *koku-minshuku-sha*. They are located in popular tourist destinations and are cheap. You may make reservations for rooms in a hotel, *ryokan* or *minshuku* through the Japan Travel Bureau (JTB) which also sells regional package tours. You may also call the Tourist Information Centre (TIC) for assistance. Their centre is at Narita Airport: Tel (0476) 328711; in Tokyo they are not far from the Yurakucho Station at 6-6 Yusakucho 1-chome, Chiyoda-ku: Tel (03) 5021461.

WHERE TO EAT AND DRINK IN TOKYO

Eating Out

To eat out in Japan it is useful to know the names of several dishes. Familiarise yourself with the names of popular dishes before you make the rounds of the restaurants. You may eat in your hotel, in the side streets or at fast food shops.

Tampura is a deep fried food and usually comprises fish, prawns and vegetables. *Saba* refers to thin noodles which are made of buckwheat. Noodles may be eaten Chinese-style (mixed with leafy vegetables, seafood and soy sauce). Thicker wheat-flour noodles are *Udon* while *Somen* are thin noodles which are eaten cold in summer. *Sushi* is vinegared pressed rice which is served in little pieces. It is topped with finely sliced pieces of raw fish dipped in soy sauce. *Unagi*, an expensive local favourite, is grilled eel. *Sukiyaki* is a meat dish popularised by the Americans. It is a dish comprising meat and vegetables cooked with sugar and soy sauce.

Some restaurants advertise their specialities by displaying lifelike plastic replicas in their show cases. Look at the prices before ordering. Ask for the menu in English.

Drinking Out

When you visit a Japanese bar be prepared to pay a lot for your drinks. You will be served by a hostess who will be willing to accept drinks and then present you with a bill that will empty your wallet. At a Japanese cabaret you will be entertained by floor shows often performed by topless dancers. You will be encouraged to drink Japanese whisky, *Sake* or soft drinks that may cost you a day's earnings. It is best to visit these establishments on a night tour. For about US$60 you will get to see these places safely with a tour guide. The bus will pick you up and return you to your hotel.

A *Karaoke* (empty orchestra) bar provides an opportunity for the guests to sing along with pre-recorded songs on tapes. There are no hostesses. Newer establishments are

5

Pedestrians heading for restaurants in Tokyo.

equipped with laser video discs, spotlights and screens. Most tourists who must have their liquor, buy their rations in the plane at duty-free prices. These become prized possessions for informal get-togethers at their hotels.

Entertainment in Kabuku-Cho

Not to be overlooked by night revellers is the Kabuku-Cho, the haunt of young working people. Its 90,000 sq metre area has over 4000 bars, clubs, discotheques and restaurants. Some are 24-hour establishments.

Shopping in Ameyoko

Ameyoko is located between the Ueno and Okachimachi subway stations. It is a lively urban market with over 3000 stalls and shops selling food, fashionable clothes, Japanese pearls and leather goods at affordable prices.

WHERE TO SHOP IN TOKYO

Department stores in Shinjuku.

Bunkuro-Cho and Yokoyama-Cho

This district is famous for its wholesalers whose shops are stocked with clothing bargains, toys, stationery and leather goods. They were so exclusive at one time that they only catered for wholesalers. They are now open to customers from all walks of life.

Ginza and Chic Shopping

The distinctive landmarks of this chic shopping district include the Mitsukoshi department store, the Wako building, the Sony building and the Honkyu Department Store. Jewellers, boutiques and restaurants here do brisk business. On Sunday afternoons and on public holidays, strollers and window-shoppers take over the Ginza when it is closed to traffic. It is a good place to relax and have a drink under a coloured parasol at a street cafe. At night the Ginza is aglow with neon lights as the famous San-Ai and Sapporo buildings

6

light up to reveal bars, clubs and small restaurants along the side streets.

Discount Camera Shops

Tourists believe that a camera is cheaper in Japan than at home. Myth or otherwise there are ready buyers for the latest models. In Tokyo the discount camera stores are not far from the East and West exits of Shinjuku Station. Their range of merchandise includes photographic equipment, watches, audio and video equipment and TV sets — at bargain prices.

Electronic Goods

Akihabara is often advertised as the bargain centre for electrical and electronic goods. This one kilometre stretch of stores is well stocked with all kinds of household and audio-visual appliances.

Sony Building

Not far from the Ginza's Sukiyabashi intersection is the Sony building. The best of Sony's products is on display in attractive showcases. Several floors of this building house Japanese creations in electrical and electronic goods alongside imported goods. For the tired or hungry shopper, Maxim's de Paris restaurant is also in the building.

Fashion Mecca

Takeshita Dori (Street) is a fashion Mecca for the youth of Tokyo. It is located between Harajuku Station's Takeshita's exit and Meiji Dori. Daily crowds of youngsters, mostly young ladies, patronise the fashion boutiques, hamburger stands, ice-cream parlours and inexpensive accessory stores.

Tokyo's Champs Elysees

Yet another meeting place for trendy people is Omotesando which extends eastward from the Harajuku Station to Aoyama Dori (Street). This beautiful avenue is flanked by boutiques, cafes and restaurants. The young and old gather in this popular area to shop and savour the festive atmosphere, particularly at weekends.

Shibuya Street

Considered a centre for the fashionable set, this street boasts a large number of boutiques and two large department stores. They are the Parco and Seibu Department Stores. They are popular with young Japanese women.

Department Stores

The following 12 department stores are within reach of each other by taxi. Many of them are in the Morunaochi and Ginza districts.

	Names	Tel Nos
1	Daimaru, Tokyo Station	212-8011
2	Hankyu, Sukiyabashi	575-2231
3	Hankyu, Yurakucho	575-2233
4	Isetan, Shinjuku	352-1111
5	Keio, Shinjuku	342-2111
6	Matsuya, Asakusa	842-1111
7	Matsuya, Ginza	567-1211
8	Matsuzakaya, Ginza	572-1111
9	Matsuzakaya, Ueno	832-1111
10	Mitsukoshi, Ginza	562-1111
11	Mitsukoshi, Ikebukuro	987-1111
12	Mitsukoshi, Nihombashi	241-3311

The following are other department stores which are worth visiting.

	Names	Tel Nos
1	Mitsukoshi Shinjuku	354-1111
2	Odakyu, Shinjuku	342-1111
3	Printemps, Ginza	567-0077
4	Seibu, Ikebukuro	981-0111
5	Seibu, Shibuya	462-0111
6	Seibu, Yurakucho	286-0111
7	Sogo, Yurakucho	284-6711
8	Takashimaya, Nihombashi	211-4111
9	Tobu, Ikebukuro	981-2211
10	Tokyu, Nihombashi	211-0511
11	Tokyu, Shibuya	477-3111
12	Wako	562-1111

7

If You Need Help

We hope the following information will be useful to you.

Hospitals	Tel No
1 International Catholic Hospital	95-11111
2 Ishikawa Clinic	479-0081
At night	401-6340
3 Red Cross Medical Centre	400-1311
4 St Luke's International Hospital	541-5151

Emergencies	Tel No
Ambulance	119
Fire	119
Police	110
Overseas Calls	0051
(Use green phone.)	
Telegrams	344-5151
(Not accepted from public phones.)	

Domestic Transportation
1 All Nippon Airline (ANA) 552-6311
2 Japan Air Lines 456-2111
3 Japan Air System Co Ltd 747-8111
4 Fujita Kanko 433-5151 (travel agency)
5 East Japan Railway Co 212-4441

Tourist Information
1 Japan National Tourist Organization (UNTO)
2 Tourist Information Centre (TIC)
For both organisations call:
Kyoto Tel (075) 371-0480
Narita Tel (0475) 32-8711
Tokyo Tel (03) 502-1461

Travel Phone
Travel Phone is a service that offers travel information and helps those who have language problems. Outside Tokyo and Kyoto, the toll-free No is 0120-222-800 for information on eastern Japan and 0120-444-800 for information on western Japan. If you are calling from Kyoto, the number is 371-5649. Within Tokyo, call 502-1461. The area code for Tokyo is (03) if you dial Tokyo from another city.

Booking Your Tour
Most hotels have brochures on tours. They also act as agents for tour organisations and will be glad to advise you. Make your bookings with them to get to any of the above places.

8

List of Embassies in Tokyo

Countries	Tel Nos	Countries	Tel Nos
America	224-5000	Haiti	486-7070
Afghanistan	407-7900	Honduras	409-1150
Algeria	711-2661	Hungary	476-6061
Arab Emirates	478-0650	India	262-2391
Argentina	592-0321	Indonesia	441-4201
Australia	435-0971	Iran	446-8011
Austria	451-8281	Iraq	423-1727
Bangladesh	442-1501	Ireland	263-0695
Belgium	262-0191	Israel	264-0911
Bolivia	499-5442	Italy	453-5291
Brazil	404-5211	Jordan	580-5856
Bulgaria	465-1021	Kenya	723-4006
Burma	441-9291	Kiribati	201-3487
Canada	408-2101	Korea (Republic)	452-7611
Central Africa	460-8341	Kuwait	455-0361
Chile	452-7561	Laos	408-1166
China (PRC)	403-3380	Lebanon	580-1227
Colombia	440-6451	Liberia	499-2451
Costa Rica	486-1812	Libya	477-0701
Cote D'lvoire	499-7021	Luxembourg	265-9621
Cuba	449-7511	Madagascar	446-7252
Czechoslovakia	400-8122	Malaysia	770-9331
Denmark	496-3001	Mexico	581-1131
Dominican (Republic)	499-6020	Mongolia	469-2088
Ecuador	499-2800	Morocco	478-3271
Egypt	770-8021	Nepal	705-5558
El Salvador	499-4461	The Netherlands	431-5126
Ethiopia	585-3151	New Zealand	467-2271
Fiji	587-2038	Nicaragua	499-0400
Finland	442-2231	Nigeria	468-5531
France	473-0171	Norway	440-2611
Gabon	448-9540	Oman	402-0877
Germany (Dem Rep)	585-5404	Pakistan	454-4861
Germany (Fed Rep)	473-0151	Panama	499-3741
Ghana	409-3861	Papua New Guinea	454-7801
Greece	403-0871	Paraguay	447-7496
Guatemala	400-1820	Singapore	586-9111
Guinea	769-0451		

9

List of Airlines

Aeroflot Soviet		Japan Air System	563-1515
Airlines	434-9681	Japan Asia Airways	455-7511
Air France	475-1511	KLM Royal Dutch	
Air India	214-1981	Airlines	211-5323
Air Lanka	573-4264	Korean Air Lines	211-3311
Air New Zealand	287-1641	Lufthansa German	
Air Pacific	593-7030	Airlines	580-2121
Alitalia Italian		Malaysian Airline	
Airlines	580-2181	System	503-5961
All Nippon Airways	272-1212	Northwest Airlines	593-7000
American Airlines	214-2111	Pakistan International	
Austrian Airlines	582-2231	Airlines	216-6511
Bangladesh Biman	593-1252	Philippine Air	
British Airways	593-8811	Lines	593-2421
Canadian Airlines		Qantas Airways	212-1351
International	281-7426	Sabena Belgian	
Cathay Pacific		World Airlines	585-6151
Airways	504-1531	Scandinavian Airlines	
China Airlines	436-1661	System	503-8101
Civil Aviation		Singapore Airlines	213-3431
Administration		Swiss Air	212-1016
of China	505-2021	Thai Airways	
Continental Airlines	214-2623	International	503-3311
Delta Air Lines	213-8781	Trans World	
Egypt Air	211-4521	Airlines	212-1477
Finnair	222-6801	Turkish Airlines	595-2901
Garuda Indonesian		United Air Lines	817-4411
Airways	593-1181	UTA French	
Iberia Airlines		Airlines	593-0773
of Spain	582-3831	Varig Brazilian	
Iran National		Airlines	211-6751
Airlines	586-2101	Virgin Atlantic	
Iraqi Airways	264-5501	Airways	435-8330
Japan Air Lines	457-1111		

For airport information, please call:
Narita (0476) 32-2800; Haneda (03) 747-8010.

JAPAN AND ITS NEIGHBOURS

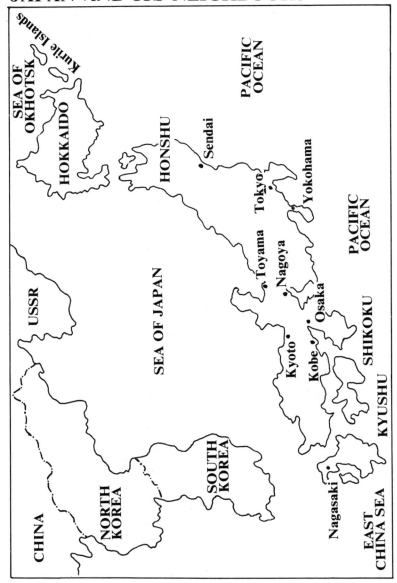

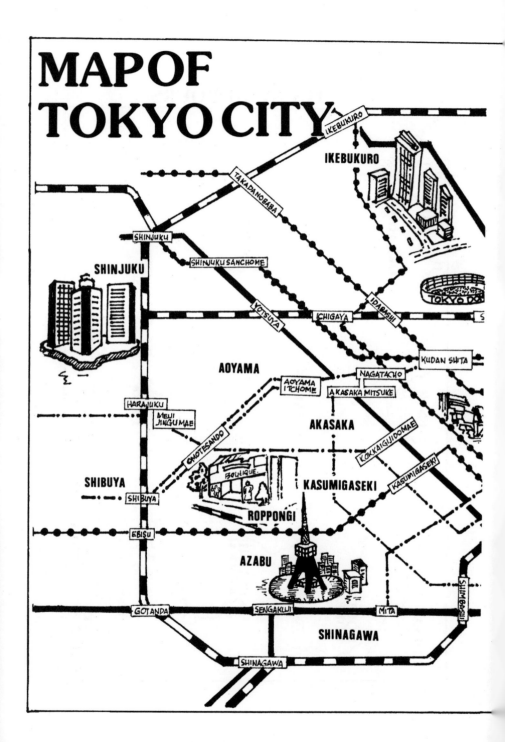

MAP OF TOKYO CITY

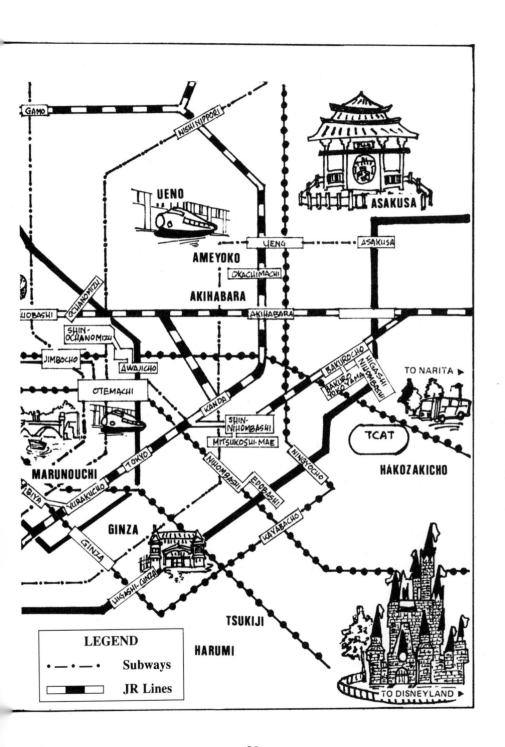

GAMO

NISHI NIPPORI

UENO

AMEYOKO

UENO

ASAKUSA

ASAKUSA

OKACHIMACHI

AKIHABARA

AKIHABARA

OCHANOMIZU

UOBASHI

SHIN-
OCHANOMIZU

JIMBOCHO

AWAJICHO

BAKUROCHO

HIGASHI
NIHOMBASHI

TO NARITA ▶

BAKURO
YOKOYAMA

OTEMACHI

KANDA

SHIN-
NIHOMBASHI

TCAT

MITSUKOSHI-MAE

TOKYO

NIHOMBASHI

EDOBASHI

NINGYOCHO

HAKOZAKICHO

MARUNOUCHI

BIYA

YURAKUCHO

KAYABACHO

GINZA

GINZA

HIGASHI-GINZA

TSUKIJI

HARUMI

TO DISNEYLAND ▶

LEGEND

• — • — • Subways

JR Lines

99

For Lasting Impressions

To leave lasting impressions as a tourist, businessman or goodwill ambassador, you have to speak and possibly write some Japanese. Prepare for the opportunities that will come your way by learning Japanese soon with Europhone. We have three Japanese courses to offer you. They differ in content and extent. The smaller packages offer less materials than the bigger ones.

Stages	Contents	Net Price
I Eurotone Classic	4 Cassettes, 3 Books Optional 3 Months Correspondence Service	S$125/US$65
II Europack	6 Cassettes, 3 Books Optional 6 Months Correspondence Service	S$209/US$110
III Europhone	8 Cassettes, 4 Books Optional 12 Months Correspondence Service	S$399/US$189

Romaji and Kanji

All the above courses begin with simple lessons and progress to higher levels. The instruction is in English; Romanised Japanese (Romaji) is taught. For the study of Japanese characters, an optional book on characters is available. For Singapore and Malaysia, postage is free. For other destinations, please refer to the Order Form.

How To Order

Please use the Order Form and forward it with your bankdraft, Money Order or cheque made payable to the *Europhone Language Institute*.

Europhone Language Institute

HIGHER STANDARD LANGUAGE COURSES

1. **EUROTONE CLASSIC COURSES** — (*Short Course*)
   We hope you have found this short language course interesting and helpful. It is a good beginning that will improve your career and business prospects.

2. **EUROPACK COURSES** — (*Medium Length Course*)
   Europack courses are for two groups:
   (a) Those who have completed a **Eurotone** Classic course and want to progress to the next standard.
   (b) Those who have found **Eurotone** Classic courses too simple. You will be supplied with more cassettes and a bigger package of higher standard study materials when you obtain a **Europack** course. These courses are available at our offices in Penang, Kuala Lumpur and Singapore. Write to us or telephone us.

3. **EUROPHONE COURSES** — (*Complete Course*)
   For those who want the best language courses in quality and service, we offer **Europhone Courses**. They comprise 8 cassettes, 3 books and one year of free written **Advisory Service**. An optional **Correspondence Service** provides supervision of your studies through tests. There is a **Proficiency Certificate** at the end of the course for a service charge.

YOU HAVE A CHOICE
The above is the widest range of courses in the market. There is a course to suit your budget as well as your level of study.

OUR GUARANTEE
This is our 20th year in the market. Our experience and expertise are your guarantee to success in your language studies. See us today for your language needs.

Director of Studies

LIST OF EUROTONE BOOK-CASSETTES

Book-Cassettes

1	Simple Arabic	10	Simple Mandarin
2	Bahasa Arab	11	Simple Thai
3	Simple English*	12	Simple Tamil
4	Simple English**	13	Simple Hindi
5	Simple English***	14	Simple French
6	Simple Indonesian	15	Simple German
7	Simple Malay	16	Simple Spanish
8	Simple Japanese	17	Simple Italian
9	Simple Korean		

*   With Malay translation
**   With Mandarin translation
*** With Japanese translation

ABOUT THE BOOK-CASSETTES

1 A Book-Cassette comprises a *Simple* language book and a 60 minute cassette which contains the recording of ten Lessons in the native language. Each sentence or phrase is followed by a pause for the learner to speak in imitation of the teacher. This provides essential practice in the spoken language.

2 The book contains the same ten Lessons as in the cassette. Each Lesson has its Vocabulary list and Explanations of grammar to help the student construct his own sentences for meaningful conversations.

3 A Book-Cassette comprising a quality book and a 60 minute cassette of recordings is priced at US$27 (S$45)including surface mail to any destination, please add US$10, for air mail.

Please use the Order Form.

LIST OF EUROTONE CLASSIC COURSES

Item	Courses
1	French Classic
2	German Classic
3	Spanish Classic
*4	Italian Classic
5	English Classic**
6	English Classic†
7	English Classic***
8	Mandarin Classic
*9	Japanese Classic
10	Korean Classic
11	Malay Classic
12	Indonesian Classic
13	Tamil Classic
14	Thai Classic

Services

1 Correction of your Workbook and its return with our corrections, comments and evaluation for all items except those marked thus (*).

2 Award of Certificate of Progress on fulfilment of para 1, above.

3 Guaranteed quality cassettes and books. Defective items may be exchanged within one month of receipt.

** With Mandarin translation
*** With Japanese translation

† With Malay translation

ABOUT THE COURSES

1 Every course has been researched, written and recorded by experts with graduate qualifications in their native language.

2 As the courses are for self-study, every consideration has been given to make them complete. Each lesson includes, a narrative passage or dialogue, translations, bilingual vocabulary, grammar, exercises, answers and cassettes for the practice of the spoken language.

3 The course materials comprise 4-cassettes, 3 books packaged in a handy carrying case. They cost only S$150 (US$90). Packing and surface mail cost US$15; for airmail please add US$25.

Please use the Order Form.

LIST OF EUROPACK COURSES

Item	Europack Courses	Services
1	Arabic with English	1 Correction of your
2	Arabic with Malay	Workbook and its
3	English with Malay*	return with our
4	English with Mandarin*	comments and
5	English with Japanese	evaluation is provided
6	French with English*	for items marked thus (*).
7	German with English	2 Award of a Certificate of
8	Hokkien with English*	Proficiency on completion
9	Japanese with English*	of these courses (*).
10	Mandarin with English	3 Free despatch by surface
11	Malay with English*	mail of your course in
12	Thai with English	Singapore or Malaysia.
13	Korean with English	

ABOUT THE COURSES

1 Every course has been researched, written and recorded by experts with graduate qualifications in their native language.

2 As the courses are for self-study, every consideration has been given to make them complete. Each lesson includes, a narrative passage or dialogue, translations, bilingual vocabulary, grammar, exercises, answers and cassettes for the practice of the spoken language, backed by two decades of know-how catering to learners' needs.

3 Many other unlisted language courses (some with eight cassettes) are available at our offices. Please write or visit our showrooms in Singapore (Tel 3373617) or Kuala Lumpur (Malaysia) Tel 2981685.

4 In all courses, the foreign language is taught through the medium of English except when otherwise stated.

5 A Europack course includes 4 to 6 cassettes, 3 books in a carrying case and the supporting services mentioned above. A Europack course costs US$175, see inner back cover. Please add US$15 for surface mail or US$45 for air mail despatch.

Please use the Order Form

ORDER FORM B

Manager
Europhone Language Institute
No 04-33 Peninsula Shopping Centre
Singapore 0617
Tel: 3373617, Fax (65) 3374506

Name & Address of Purchaser

Name _____
Address _____
_____
_____

Dear Sir

We wish to order the books/book-/cassettes/language courses listed below and enclose a crossed Cheque* / Money Order* / Bankdraft for $_____ .

* Delete as appropriate

Signature & Date

Items	State Chosen Language in Column				Unit Cost $	Qty	Total Cost $
	Europack Course	Eurotone Classic	Eurotone Book-Cassette	Others			

Payment may be made in US or Singapore dollars. $_____

Remarks _____
_____
_____

Notes
Book-Cassettes are described in the inside front cover and cost S$45 (US$27) including surface mail. Please add US$10 for air mail postage.
Eurotone Classic Courses are described in the book (see Contents page) and cost US$90. Please add US$25 for air mail postage or US$15 for surface mail.
Europack Courses are described in the inside back cover and cost US$175. Please add US$45 for air mail postage or US$15 for surface mail.
Travel Guide to Japan, (*Focus on Tokyo*) in cassette form costs US$10. For air mail please add US$5. The complete book and cassette cost US$15; For air mail please add US$15; for surface mail US$5.

NOTES

NOTES

NOTES